DO–IT–YOURSELF
a basic manual

Tony Wilkins has spent most of his working life closely involved with the subject of do-it-yourself. He joined the staff of Britain's first d-i-y magazine, 'Handyman', in 1953 as its feature editor. He then moved to 'Do It Yourself, the Home Improvement magazine' in 1957 shortly after its inception and is now the editor.

He has written many books on related subjects including *Enjoy Decorating Your Home* (Nelson), *Beginners' Guide to Do-it-yourself* (Pelham), *Hammer it home* (BBC), *Guide to Home Decorating* (Newnes-Butterworth), *Home Repair and Maintenance* (Newnes-Butterworth), *Home Improvements* (Newnes-Butterworth) and *House Repairs* in the Teach Yourself series. He has also appeared on television and is known for his connection with the BBC Radio 4 'Tuesday Call' – a phone-in programme dealing with listeners' problems.

DO–IT–YOURSELF
a basic manual

Tony Wilkins

Illustrations by
Bill Thacker

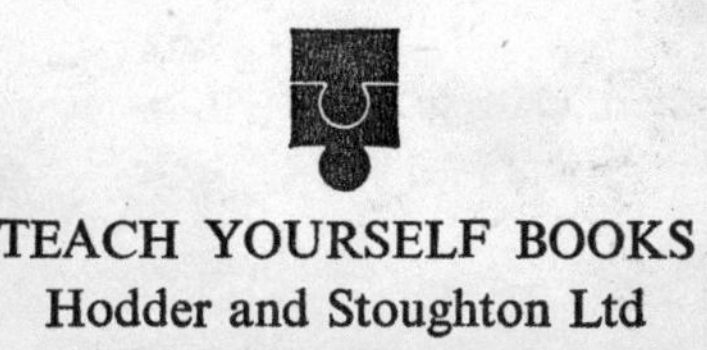

TEACH YOURSELF BOOKS
Hodder and Stoughton Ltd

Contents

Introduction   1

1   Tools and Hardware   5

2   Materials you will need   23

3   Jobs about the House   45

4   Domestic Emergencies   111

5   Useful Hints and Tips   121

Glossary of Terms   133
Index   149

Introduction

At one time, doing more than general spring cleaning – and perhaps a little decorating – was considered best left to the adventurous. Plumbing and electricity were there for professionals to take care of, and 'calling a man in' was part of our way of life.

Over the past twenty years there has been a quiet revolution, and people from all walks of life have found themselves with far more responsibility for their home maintenance and repairs. Skilled tradesmen willing to tackle the small fiddly repair jobs are difficult to find – and if you do find a good one you may have to wait weeks for a call. Labour charges have risen enormously, and even small jobs can cost a lot when charges are made for visits, for taking away and returning appliances, and even for diagnosing faults.

Having tried tackling jobs themselves, many have found that if you follow the 'rules', it is not that difficult after all. In fact there can be a very considerable sense of achievement and satisfaction when you say, 'Well, actually I did it myself.'

Of course, there will always be areas best left to the professional, and it is not the purpose of this book to lead you into trouble. Where there may be danger, where the work could be very heavy and demanding, or where you may just not have the time, I will endeavour to warn you and point you in the right direction for help. My experience over many years is that you will always find many helpful experts – in stores, factories and in the many professional associations. People are always ready to offer a word of advice, or offer literature or contacts, but what they don't like is being asked to help clean up a mess when you've had a go at a job and failed! With every job, make sure you understand what to do, what you need and where the snags lie before you do anything. In that way you will avoid the pitfalls.

Treat home maintenance and repair work as something about which you will never finish learning. Keep a scrap book, and jot in it any hints and tips you pick up; useful cuttings from magazines and newspapers; trade contacts, addresses of suppliers of unusual materials, colour cards, quotes for jobs – and so on. You will find such reference invaluable and it will smooth your path.

One essential for success is an adequate kit of tools, for having the right tool for the job can transform a situation. Many jobs which seem complicated become simple when the right tool is applied, and money spent on good quality equipment is never wasted.

Chapter 1 deals with this subject in detail, but if you feel you want further advice, don't be afraid to ask an experienced assistant in a good tool shop. He can show you the tools, let you handle them and help you choose.

There may be jobs where it is uneconomical to buy tools when the work may never be repeated. In this case, go to your local hire shop. You may find it worthwhile to hire equipment for a limited period. This calls for careful advance planning so you don't have to keep the equipment too long. Remember, the longer you keep it, the more it will cost.

Another important point is to get to know the materials with which you intend to work. Read any instruction leaflets very carefully – then file them away in your reference book. This particularly applies to items made of plastics, for there are so many now, all with varying characteristics. It also applies to paints and adhesives: two very confusing areas for the beginner.

And the same rule applies to new tools and appliances. Read the instructions carefully, then file them away for future reference. If there is a service manual or parts list, it is vital to keep these against the day you have to order replacement parts. It is far easier to quote a reference number than to try and describe a part over the phone!

If the introduction has not put you off, may I say I hope you find this book useful. I wish you success in every d-i-y venture you undertake.

Tony Wilkins
1980

1

Tools and Hardware

A stroll round a modern tool shop can be a bewildering experience. How does one ever begin to choose from the hundreds of items displayed? I think we must accept at the outset that it is impossible to list the 'ideal' tool kit, for interests and tastes vary considerably. The most I can do is select a number of tools which I feel will be best suited to a beginner – and then leave it to you to expand your kit as you become more proficient and more ambitious.

Please bear one golden rule in mind. Each tool is designed for a specific job, and it should be kept for that job. For example a screwdriver makes a very poor chisel. A chisel very quickly becomes blunted if it is used for lifting floor tacks. And a wood saw cuts nails very badly! Don't abuse your tools. Treat them with respect; keep them clean and sharp, and they will give you a lifetime of faithful service.

Also, always be safety conscious. Tools correctly used are not dangerous, but it is very easy to create a situation which leads to an accident. For example, always keep you hands behind the direction of travel of a cutting blade – whether it be chisel or knife (*Figure 1*). When using tools which cause the chips to fly, protect your eyes with safety goggles. Always anchor work firmly when sawing or planing.

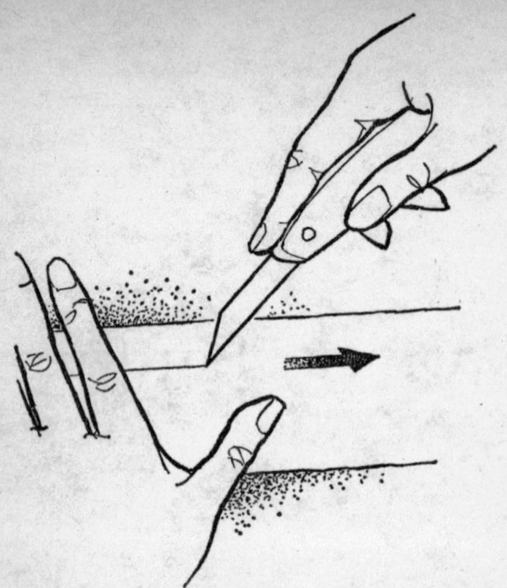

KEEP YOUR HAND BEHIND THE DIRECTION
OF TRAVEL OF ANY CUTTING TOOL

Figure 1

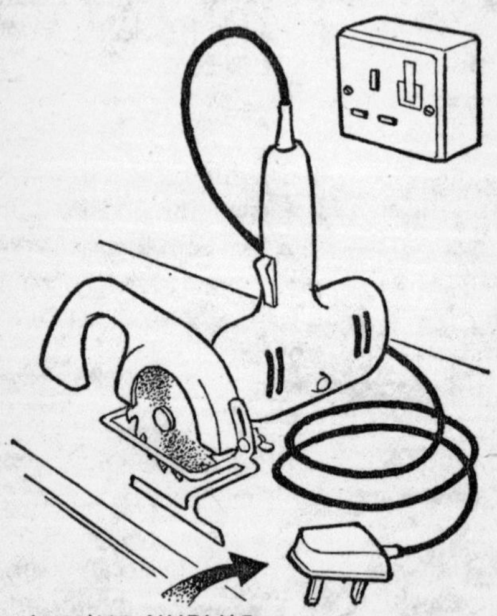

ALWAYS UNPLUG
YOUR TOOLS WHEN YOU LEAVE THEM

Figure 2

Take great care with power tool equipment, and always unplug a tool even if you are only leaving it for a moment (*Figure 2*). This is most important when there are small inquisitive children around. Anticipate dangers – and you will never have cause for regret!

Work surface

There are many cases where you need a good, firm surface to work on. This can be a sturdy old kitchen table, a work bench, or a modern folding bench (*Figure 3*). Whatever you choose, it

Figure 3

shouldn't move when you work on it. Don't rely on your best kitchen table, for you will be sure to bruise or cut it in due course.

Holding things firm and still

It is impossible to hold work steady with a hand while sawing, shaping or drilling. You get poor results – and there is always a risk of hurting yourself. You need a vice which clamps to the bench and then into which your work may be held while you work. You can have a woodworking vice which is permanently fixed to a table or bench, and this has wood jaws to grip the work (*Figure 4*). Wood is ideal as it won't bruise things held in it. Some

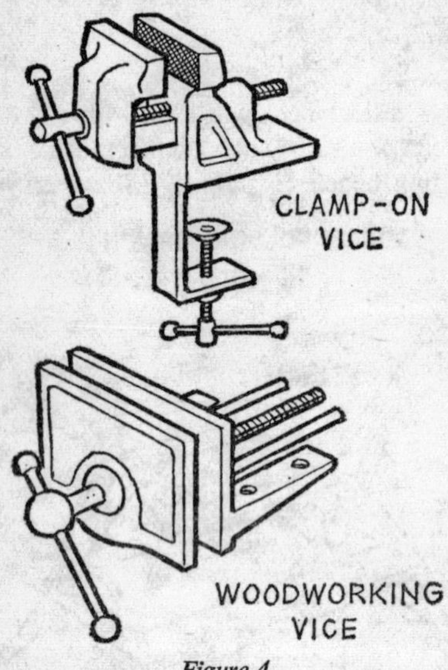

Figure 4

vices are all metal, but you will find drilled holes in the jaws, through which you can put screws to hold plates of wood.

Some modern clamp-on vices have a choice of jaw facings. You can have grooved metal for holding metal items, or you can fit rubber-faced jaws for holding soft woods and soft or decorative metals which would be marked by metal jaws. A vee-shaped groove cut in the jaw will help you hold circular material such as pipe or dowel rod.

As well as a vice, it is wise to invest in a couple of G cramps (*Figure 5*). The name comes from the basic shape, and the cramp can be used for holding materials to the bench where you want them to lie flat. Cramps can also be used for holding items to-

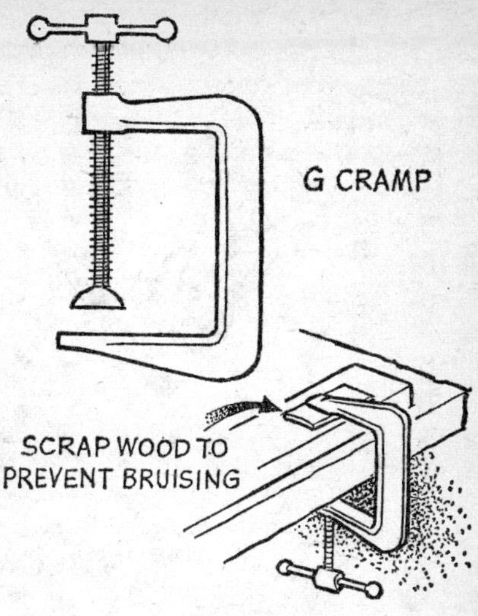

Figure 5

gether while they are worked on, or while glue sets. And if your main interest is craftwork you can get miniature cramps designed to hold very small items.

Now let us look at some basic tools (*Figure 6*).

Measuring

Steel rule This will give you accurate results. Don't use an old school ruler. Buy a rule with both metric and Imperial measures. Then you have a ready conversion from one system to the other merely by reading across.

Steel tape Get one at least 3m (10 ft) long. The little hook at the end is meant to move slightly, as this compensates for whether you are measuring internal or external surfaces. Some more sophisticated tapes have a window in the top through which you can read off your dimensions. Don't use a dressmaking cloth tape, it is not accurate enough.

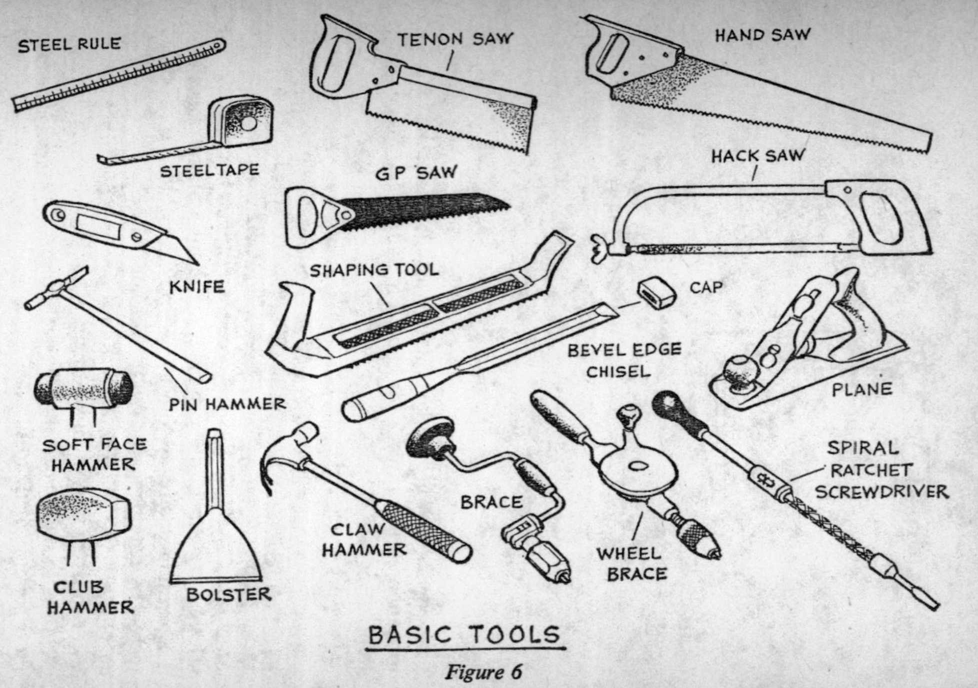
STEEL RULE
STEEL TAPE
TENON SAW
GP SAW
HAND SAW
HACK SAW
KNIFE
SHAPING TOOL
CAP
BEVEL EDGE CHISEL
PLANE
PIN HAMMER
SOFT FACE HAMMER
CLUB HAMMER
BOLSTER
CLAW HAMMER
BRACE
WHEEL BRACE
SPIRAL RATCHET SCREWDRIVER
BASIC TOOLS
Figure 6

Cutting

Tenon saw This has a stiffened back to keep the blade true, and it will make accurate cuts in smaller sections of wood. It is used for making joints, and it can be used for cutting picture framing if used in conjunction with a mitre box. Get a saw about 25 cm (10 in) long.

Cross cut hand saw For larger pieces of wood and for sheet materials you need a saw without a stiffened back, as the back would get in the way. The teeth on the saw are referred to as 'points', and the more there are, the finer the cut. For general use, get a saw with seven points per 25 mm (1 in). Your tool shop will show you this in more detail.

Hacksaw If you want to cut metals you must have a hacksaw. This is a frame into which a long thin blade is fitted and is then put under tension. When you buy the saw, see that you get instructions on how to tension the blade – too loose and it will break; too tight and you will break the holes.

GP saw This is a general purpose saw designed to cut either wood or metal, so it has a very special blade. Most are also adjustable at the handle so that the blade can be angled to suit the job in hand. While very useful, it is not as accurate as the tenon saw or fine cross cut saw. The GP is very useful when tackling jobs like trimming a strip off the base of a door – where there may be hidden nails – or for cutting up second-hand wood where there may be hidden metal. A special blade is available for tree pruning.

Chisels It is debatable whether you will need them if just beginning (*see* shaping below). But if you do want to add to your kit, buy a set ranging in size from 3 mm ($\frac{1}{8}$ in) to 25 mm (1 in). Ask for bevel edge wood chisels. If you can, get a set of plastic tips to protect the cutting edges. And get a mallet with which to hit them.

Knife A good craft knife with a selection of blades in the handle is very worthwhile. Apart from standard blades, you can get one for cutting vinyl and carpet, and one for scoring laminates. Be very careful, they are surgeon-sharp! And they should be kept that way or thrown out. A blunt blade tends to slip and is potentially dangerous.

Shaping

Plane   This is another tool you may find unnecessary as a beginner, for you can buy timber ready-planed and only needing a final sanding. But if you wish to convert old timber to a given size, a plane is useful. Choose what is called a replacement blade plane which, as the name implies, does not require sharpening and honing. The blade is easy to adjust, and when it gets dull, you throw it away and put in a new one.

Shaping tools   These are invaluable for the amateur as they are far easier to use than some of the more traditional tools. The blade is perforated and has rows of chisel-edged cutting surfaces which quickly take away wood. They come in a number of shapes, which include a miniature plane and a file. Some more sophisticated models come with an adjustable handle which can convert the tool from plane to file. The shaping tools are ideal for children too as they don't cut if you rub a hand over the blade. Ask to see a wood rasp and compare its blade with a shaping tool. A version for shaping metals is also available.

Hitting

Claw hammer   The most useful all-round tool is the claw hammer. The claw is the curved bit at the back designed for pulling nails from wood.

Pin hammer   If you do handicraft work you will need a fine hammer with which to fix panel pins and tacks. The claw hammer is too clumsy, so get a pin hammer, which has a much more delicate head. The flat section at the back of the head is useful for starting small pins.

Soft-face hammer   There are occasions when using a standard hammer would damage a surface – for example, when undoing chromium plated wing nuts on a pram. For this kind of job, a soft face of rubber or plastic is ideal, for no matter how hard you hit, it will do no damage. This is also the tool for getting dents out of metal without bruising the surface. For household use, get a small one with a different hardness each end of the head.

Club hammer   This is only required if you want to break up concrete or cut paving slabs and bricks. It has a very bulky, heavy head.

To go with it, you need a steel chisel, and a wide-blade steel chisel called a bolster. And don't forget safety goggles to protect your eyes.

Drilling

Wheel brace   This is a hand-operated drilling tool, and the wheel you turn is geared to what is called a chuck. Into the chuck fits a twist drill – which is designed to drill holes in wood, plywood, chipboard and soft metals. It is worth buying a small set of twist drills in popular sizes.

Remember that for drilling holes in plaster, brick and similar materials, you need special masonry drills with hardened tips. You can't use a normal twist drill on masonry.

Brace and bit   Designed for boring holes larger than you can produce with a wheel brace, the brace has little place in a beginner's kit – apart from one use. It can be fitted with a screwdriver bit, giving you a lot of leverage. This is the ideal tool for removing very tight screws – and in fact it is very easy to apply so much pressure that you turn the head off the screw! Remember a brace is designed for bits – not drills.

Spiral ratchet driver   Although basically a screwdriver which drives by 'pumping' the handle up and down, you can buy models which are supplied with a selection of fine drills. Although they don't have a twist, they do drill very effectively, so such a driver is very useful for fine craftwork where a lot of small holes have to be made.

Driving

One thing you are sure to need is a selection of screwdrivers, and the golden rule is that the screwdriver tip must fit neatly into the slot of the screw it is to drive, with the tip as wide as the slot. So you will need three or four just to cover a normal range of slotted screws. And apart from single slot screws you will encounter some with cross-head slots which need a special screwdriver.

Figure 8 on page 19 shows the main screw types, and you will see that there are two main cross-slot types. The Phillips head screw found in older homes and appliances, and the Pozidriv-head screw. The latter is a refinement of the Phillips, designed to get a more accurate fit, and at the time of writing even this has been modified in favour of what is called the Supadriv. So you may meet Pozidriv or Supadriv. Again, note that there are different sizes of driver for different screw sizes, so you need more than one screwdriver.

One great advantage of the cross-slot is that the screwdriver tips don't slip out so easily. This makes it easier to drive the screw, and there is less likelihood of marking decorative surfaces.

So you will need:

1.   Single slot screwdrivers – two or three.
2.   Cross-slot drivers – two or three plus a Phillips driver if you encounter these screws.
3.   Short electrician's screwdriver with insulated handle for wiring plugs.

If you do fine craftwork, a useful investment is a set of watch-maker's screwdrivers in a little wallet.

As well as the normal solid handle screwdrivers, you can buy what is called a ratchet driver where the blade and handle move separately (*Figure 7*). The ratchet can be set to drive in or take out screws, and the advantage is that the screwdriver tip need never disengage from the slot. Then there is the spiral ratchet or pump-handle driver I mentioned earlier with a set of screwdriver tips and drills in the handle.

You will find you collect a few specials as you progress, such as a stubby handled driver for getting in confined spots, and an off-set driver for turning screws where you can't get above them.

Gripping and turning

Pliers For gripping objects and cutting wire.
Fine nose pliers   For holding small items and for craftwork.
Pincers   For gripping and pulling nails and tacks.
Self-grip wrench   For gripping items and locking on to them,

FINE NOSE PLIERS
PINCERS
NAIL PUNCH
PLIERS
STUBBY DRIVER
TABLE CLAMP
COUNTERSINK BIT
SPIRIT LEVEL
SURVEYOR'S TAPE
CABINET SCREWDRIVER
RATCHET DRIVER
SELF GRIP WRENCH
ADJUSTABLE SPANNER
TILE CUTTER
GLASS CUTTER
BASIC TOOLS

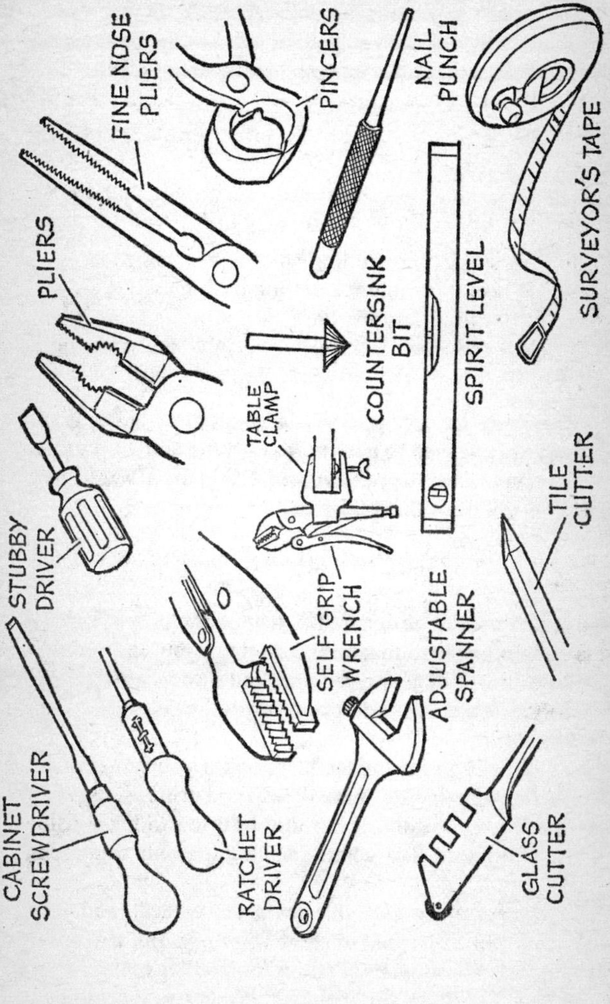

Figure 7

leaving both hands free. A special clamp-on holder is available to turn the wrench into a mini table vice.

Adjustable spanner   For undoing nuts on bolts. If you tackle plumbing work you will need a large adjustable spanner, plus a tool called a chain wrench for gripping and turning pipes.

Then there are a few items difficult to categorise:

Countersink bit   For making recesses into which screw heads will sit flush with a surface.

Spirit level   Vital when fitting shelves, hanging cupboards or starting tiling.

Nail punch   For sinking protruding nails below a surface.

Glass cutter   Wheel type only for cutting fresh glass.

Tile cutter   For scoring ceramic tiles.

Surveyor's measuring tape   For really big jobs like planning a patio or path where a short tape would be impractical.

The tools listed so far will give you a good start, but it is inevitable that you will need to add more. Painting and decorating, plus all the preparatory work involved brings in a whole new range, and we will meet these later on.

Power tools

One area which cannot be ignored is that of the power-assisted tool. It is quite possible to manage without any, but the addition of a few power tools will greatly simplify and speed up many jobs. Don't be too ambitious at the outset, but add or change as you gain experience.

Power drill   This is an invaluable help, and if you can afford it buy one with variable speed. This will help you drill holes in most materials quickly and neatly. It can also be fitted with a sanding disc, sanding drum or flap wheel for cleaning and smoothing surfaces.

Other attachments are available for a power drill, and your local tool shop will be pleased to show you these. But if you can afford it, buy one or two integral power tools where each tool has its own motor. This is by far the most efficient way of doing a job – and you don't have to keep changing attachments.

The most useful tools are the *power jigsaw*, the *circular saw* and the *orbital sander*. Again, any good tool shop will be pleased to show you these and explain their virtues.

The length of cable supplied with a power tool is never adequate, and it is well worth buying an extension cable drum into which the tool can be plugged. Always ensure that the cable is kept well out of the working area so you can't damage it.

Hire tools

There may be occasions where it just isn't cost effective to buy tools which may only be needed once or twice. In such situations it may well be wise to hire what you need from a local hire shop. They will be pleased to supply you with a leaflet giving terms of hire and costs per day and week. Bear in mind that it is cheaper if you can arrange to collect and return the items borrowed yourself. And it is most important to plan your work so you don't keep the items longer than necessary.

The variety of equipment available is extensive, including concrete mixers, steam wallpaper strippers, damp-proof course injectors, insecticide sprays, heavy duty power tools, ladders and scaffolding, roof ladders – and a whole range of garden equipment including cultivators and flame guns.

As a beginner you may feel much of the equipment mentioned is at present beyond your scope. Even so it is worth knowing of its existence for those occasions when you could call on the assistance of someone more experienced.

Practice makes perfect

As with all activities, practice breeds confidence and acceptable results, so spend time trying out your new tools on scrap materials. Cutting, shaping, drilling, smoothing – all improve with experience, and it will save you spoiling good materials when there is a job in hand.

Basic hardware

For practically all the jobs you tackle, whether new constructions or repair work, you will be amazed at the amount of hardware required, however simple it may seem. Here is just a selection.

Screws

Figure 8 shows the main types available, and a selection of most will be invaluable.

Countersunk head   This lies flush with a surface – and you need to use your countersink bit to make the right recess for it.

Round head screw   The head sits on the surface of the work.

Oval screw   Half countersunk and half exposed.

Single slot   Still the most common screw type.

Cross slot   Much easier to drive and less likely to let the screw-driver slip.

Chipboard screw   Has a special shape which holds chipboard without breaking it up.

Dome head screw   For producing a decorative finish. A little cap screws on after the screw is in place.

Self-tapping screw   This is used in sheet metal, and it will make its own grip in a hole drilled in the metal.

Clutch head screw   This has a special head which allows you to screw it up, but makes it quite impossible to undo. This is used for security purposes – such as the fixing of hasps and staples for pad-locks where you want to ensure the screws are not tampered with.

Nails

Figure 9 shows the main types and there are three main categories.

1.   Very *fine pins and nails* for delicate work and for hard woods.
2.   *Round wire nails* for rough carpentry where appearance doesn't matter too much but a good grip is required.
3.   *Oval nails*, which can be sunk into a surface, and which are far less likely to split thinner sections of wood.

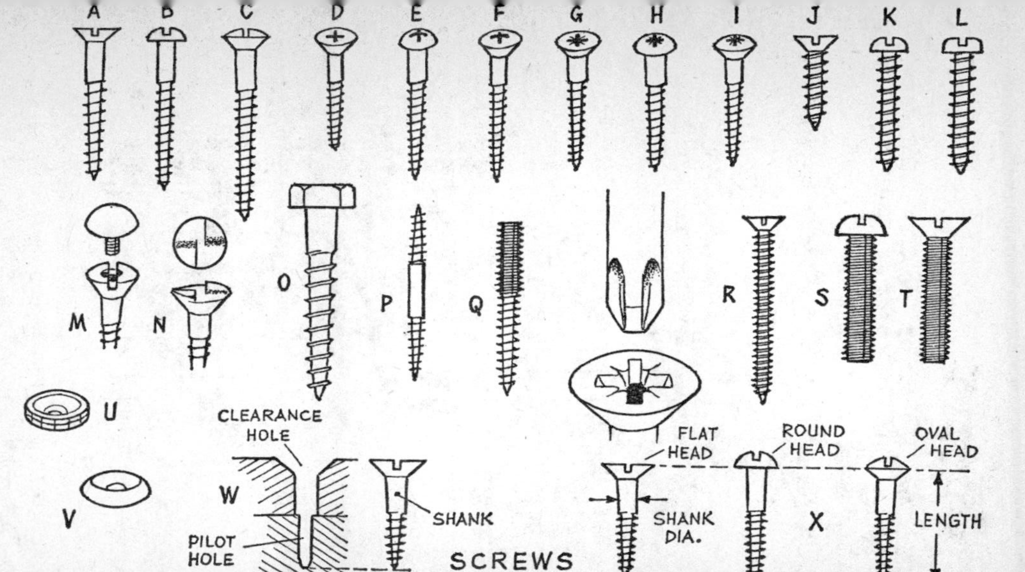

Figure 8   Key: **A**, standard flat head countersunk screw. **B**, round head screw. **C**, oval head screw. **D, E** and **F** show similar pattern screws but with Phillips cross heads. **G, H** and **I** show three examples of Pozidriv heads. **J, K** and **L** are self-tapping screws. **M**, dome head mirror screw. **N**, clutch head security screw. **O**, coach screw. **P**, dowel screw. **Q**, wood thread/metal thread dowel screw. **R**, chipboard screw. **S** and **T**, machine screw. **U**, and **V**, screw cups. **W**, method of making clearance and pilot hole, plus a recess for the countersunk head. **X**, method of measuring screw lengths.

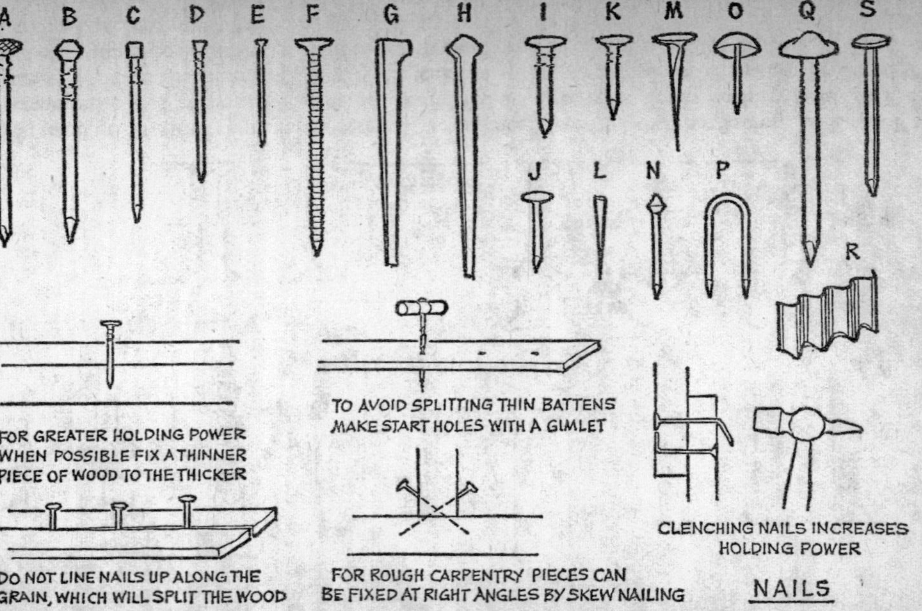

Figure 9 Key: A, wire nail. B, oval wire nail. C, lost-head wire nail. D, panel pin. E, veneer pin. F, annular ring nail. G, cut floor brad. H, cut clasp nail. I, clout nail. J, gimp pin. K, wire tack, L, sprig. M, cut tack. N, deep drive panel pin. O, brass chair nail. P, staple. Q, stack pipe nail. R, corrugated fastener or wiggle nail. S, masonry nail.

Then there are the more specialist items. Thin sheet materials need nails or tacks with large heads so the material can't pull through. *Ring nails* have serrated bodies which grip very well in soft wood like Western red cedar. *Staples* are designed to sit over wire or cable and hold it in place. Note that there is a special insulated staple for electrical work.

It pays to buy a little cabinet with plenty of drawers, and have a drawer for each type. It can save hours of selecting when actually working on a job, and it is very easy to see what you are running short of.

In locations where corrosion is a problem, you can get both screws and nails in rust-free materials. Aluminium alloy is ideal, but you will also encounter brass, galvanised metal and painted items. Aluminium seems to cost considerably more until you consider you get a lot more for a given weight as it is much lighter.

Finally, there will always be certain jobs where you need to buy specific pieces of hardware such as hinges, locks and catches. Always be sure to get these before you finalise your plan of action.

There is nothing more frustrating than starting a project, only to find that the hardware required is unobtainable or needs to be ordered specially – when a slight modification of the plan could allow you to use something freely available.

This is particularly true with special hinges you may have seen on a proprietary cabinet. They may well not be available retail – though they may be available mail-order from a specialist supplier, if you are prepared to wait. Ask first!

Also bear in mind that special items may need special screws. For example, a fine piano hinge needs very tiny screws to hold it – and a very fine screwdriver to match! One kit I purchased had a piano hinge fitted with minute Pozidriv screws. I was held up for a weekend until I could buy an extra fine screwdriver with which to drive them into the carcase of the unit.

Choose catches which are easy to fit, and preferably which offer you some simple means of adjustment after locating. That is why some items have elongated holes rather than the normal circular hole. Read the instructions carefully as to how to fit.

If a number of screws are to be used to fit a hinge or catch, secure it with just one first, then test to see that all is well. Should you have made a mistake, you still have one or two more tries in hand using the remaining holes.

Finally, remember hardware items are quite expensive these days, so whenever you are discarding units for scrap, collect any fittings, screws, pins or removable nails and store them for future use in a scrap box. Add odd items like paper clips, pieces of clock spring, brass strip, metal rod, tiny screws from old electrical fittings and metal washers. They will all come in useful one day.

2

Materials you will need

One of the most common errors when doing jobs about the house is to neglect advance planning. Most projects involve materials of some kind, so it is vital to decide what you want to use, then how much you need – then finally to make sure you have it before you start work. It all sounds so elementary, and yet it is amazing how many tasks founder on one or more of these points.

So, spend time gathering information on materials, especially leaflets which give details of coverage. And don't be afraid to ask! You are not expected to know all the answers. But do choose a time when the department is slack or the manager is free. So Saturday morning is not the ideal time!

Here are just a few guidelines. You can add from your own experience.

Paint

Remember absorbent surfaces such as bare plaster take more paint than surfaces which are merely to be repainted. Textured and relief materials also take considerably more than a smooth surface. Changing from one colour to another where there is a considerable difference may call for two coats of undercoat. Top coats have very little – if any – covering power.

When measuring up, divide surfaces into measurable rectangles then add them all together. Window frames are hard. Count a window as a solid area by multiplying width by height.

Shop around for paint, as quality materials can be bought at very considerable discounts. And buying one large can is usually less expensive than a lot of smaller ones. It also ensures that the colour is consistent, as batches can and do vary slightly. You will find the batch number on the can.

Remember also that paint coverage can vary from type to type, so don't generalise. Choose your paint, then check on the can to find the recommended coverage.

Wallcoverings

A wallpaper chart will help you estimate how many rolls you need, though bear in mind that big patterns and large repeat distances between patterns can eat up more paper than a random, small pattern. If in doubt, ask for an extra roll, then keep it sealed. If not required most shops will take it back but do check first. Ordering just one extra roll when you've run out can be tricky, for if they've not got it in stock there may be difficulty in getting one from the same batch. Remember colours can vary from batch to batch as colours are changed and different mixes are used. The batch number is shown on each roll.

If you have to accept rolls from a different batch, lose the change either side of a window where a slight change won't be apparent.

Remember that Continental papers may be different in width and length. Details should be given in the front of the pattern book and you will have to adjust your calculations. The same applies to special materials such as fabrics and grasscloths.

When using something out of the ordinary, ask for an instruction leaflet. In some cases a different paste may be necessary, and you may be advised to apply it to the wall and not the wallcovering. Very often, impervious materials like vinyls will have a fungicide added to the paste to inhibit mould growth. Vinyl cannot 'breathe' like a paper, and so mould growth is encouraged. You would be wise to use the right material, and not some leftover wallpaper paste.

Tiles

Again, manufacturers usually supply a useful chart showing how you should estimate requirements. Apart from overall areas, remember you must allow for any patterned tiles you wish to add. And in many types, you will need smooth edge tiles to finish off at the extremities, as opposed to the normal tiles which have little nibs to space the tiles apart.

Certain manufacturers are now introducing designs which need no special edge tiles. Ask for details when you are selecting in the shop.

Remember too items like accessory tiles which can be inserted – toilet roll holder, soap dish, hooks and towel rails.

Quite a number of foreign tiles, particularly for flooring, are being imported, and some are very attractive. Check these for size and coverage before you order. And ask for the recommended adhesive at the time. If the tiles will be in an exposed place, such as in a shower cabinet or on a bathroom floor, ensure that the grouting supplied will withstand damp.

Timber and boards

Try to make your plans and designs fit the sizes of material that you can buy. Strips cut off which just end up as waste can affect the overall cost of a project. This applies particularly to projects using materials like plywood or veneered chipboard. And remember if you cut a veneered board which has come with the edges covered, you will have to buy a roll of iron-on edging strip unless you can lose the cut edge behind another surface.

Now let us look at some of the more common materials you will encounter.

Paint

This is a very confusing product because what used to be easily divided into categories is now confused by additives and sales jargon. But having said that, the quality of British branded paints is excellent, and the majority of complaints received concerning paint are faults of surface and application rather than the material itself.

There are two fairly clearly defined types – gloss paint and emulsion paint, though even this has been confused by the introduction of what are called acrylic glosses. These are really glossy emulsion paints, but they don't as yet take over from the true gloss.

Gloss   Used for wooden and metal surfaces. Most are now based upon what is called alkyd resin, but you don't even need to remember that for ordering. You can get it in high gloss and some form of sheen, and all you need to remember is that gloss is easy to keep clean but it does tend to show up surface blemishes. A sheen is often more likely to show marks, but it does disguise surface blemishes. Some sheen wall finishes are easier to clean as a result of additives, such as vinyl – so it is wise to ask for details before deciding.

Thixotropic   Also known as jelly paints, these have a special ingredient which jells when the paint is left standing, but liquefies when disturbed. They are really designed for the amateur, as they don't splash, can be applied quite thickly without dripping, and give good coverage. Some are referred to as one-coat paints as they need no undercoat, but it is wise to remember that when changing from one colour to another you may still need two coats if the under-colour is not to 'grin' through. This will also give a more professional finish.

Remember that you do not stir it before use – if you stir jelly paint it thins and goes runny. Leave it to gel again before using to avoid drips. Just dip the brush in the jelly. Has it any disadvantages? Well, I feel it doesn't brush out as well as a standard gloss, so you often don't get such a smooth mirror finish. When you become proficient at painting, I think you should graduate to a standard gloss paint.

Paints with additives   There are now many paints which include additives to improve their performance in some way. Some do and some are no more than an advertising gimmick. So spend time talking in your paint shop. You will discover *vinyl*, which can make a paint tough and easy to clean; *silicone*, which improves its dirt-shedding properties, *polyurethane*, which toughens the surface and helps resist abrasion, *mica*, which thickens it and fills gaps on exterior surfaces, *nylon fibre*, which adds strength and bridges gaps.

A true vinyl is good for walls, and you can paint over vinyl wallcoverings with it if you really want to. A true polyurethane is extremely tough though easily chipped on soft surfaces. It is ideal for metalwork – such as garage doors. A masonry paint with nylon fibre is ideal for an exterior wall which has fine hairline cracks. It will hide them beautifully.

Emulsion paint   Used for wall surfaces. This needs little description except to say it is water-based and thus sensitive to frost. And it comes in both exterior and interior qualities. Make sure if you are treating outside walls you have a material which is suitable.

This is one area where you get what you pay for. Very cheap emulsions have poor covering power and they don't spread well or last long. It pays to buy a well-known brand every time.

Enamel   This is a very high quality paint where the pigments are finely ground. They are expensive, but the results you can achieve are well worth the expense. They are used mainly for painting whitewood and smaller items of furniture, and it is interesting to note that it is one of the very few paints which can be applied to bare wood without primer or undercoat. You can get excellent results by dipping small items.

They are also used for painting models, and I'm sure you have seen the small tins in a wide variety of colours for decorating model aircraft, vehicles and soldiers.

Specialist paints   There are many materials which don't fall into any simple category, but which have been designed for a specific job. Masonry paints include those made with sand or cement as well as the emulsions with special additives. Then you can buy anti-condensation paint which absorbs a certain amount of moisture and contains a fungicide to prevent mould growth.

There are *fire-retardant paints*, rather resembling emulsion but with the ability to form an insulating barrier if heat is applied. This is an ideal decorative material for expanded polystyrene tiles (*See* also p. 67).

Then there are metallic *heat-resisting paints* in a limited range of colours, designed to withstand higher temperatures than most.

There are tough *rubber-based floor paints* for covering concrete floors or floor tiles.

And there are special *rust-inhibiting paints* for protecting metal-work exposed to the weather.

If you have some special need, consult your local paint shop and see what they have to offer.

Aerosol paints   A whole range of finishes is available in pressurised cans, and for certain jobs they can be a great help. Wrought-iron work, perforated screens, Lloyd loom furniture and other textured surfaces are easily covered.

However, as the paint has to come out of a minute nozzle, it has to be very thin – so you don't get much coverage. You must be prepared to build up coat on coat. And you can't tell how much there is in a can, so it is hard to estimate how much to buy. You must keep the nozzle immaculately clean or nothing will come out at all.

Lacquers   These are high quality paints in dense colours with a quick drying solvent, which makes them ideal for touching up work on surfaces like car bodywork and household appliances. Again you must be prepared to apply in thin layers and build up coat on coat, or you will get runs.

Associated materials

Remember that paints are principally the visible decorative surface of a protective layer, and other things have to go underneath. These include:

Knotting   A special shellac-based product which you apply over bare knots in timber to stop the resin bleeding out and spoiling your paintwork.

Primer   A special paint designed to clog the grain of a surface and seal it, and afford a key for a following coat. All bare surfaces must be primed unless otherwise stated. You will find primers designed for specific surfaces such as timber, metal or plaster. But you will also find universal primers which can be used on any bare surface.

Undercoat This is the layer of a paint system which helps change a colour and apply body to the paint. It is high in pigment for this reason. It is wise to match the undercoat to the top coat, and use the recommended colour for any given colour on a colour card.

Remember that top coat gloss has very little covering power. It can be almost transparent – but very tough.

Colour mixing machines There is a gradual tendency to change to special machines which mix your paint to order, based on a coding system. This helps the paint stockist as it cuts down the number of cans he needs on his shelves. And it helps you as it gives an almost limitless choice of colours and shades. It is wise to make sure you order enough for the job in hand, in case you get slight colour variation between batches.

Stains and seals If you want to change the colour of a natural piece of wood, perhaps to match existing furniture, you can do it with a wood stain. But it is wise to experiment first as the dry colour sometimes looks darker than expected.

You will find there are three main types – water-based, spirit-based and oil-based. The easiest to use is the oil-based one. It penetrates well, is easy to spread, is quick drying, and does not raise the grain of the wood. Remember the stain has only coloured the wood, and it is not a decorative finish. That has to be applied over the top.

You can also change the colour of wood by using a polyurethane seal which contains a colorant, and this both colours and decorates at the same time. While very attractive, remember that if more than one coat is applied, you get a successively darker finish. And if the coating is scratched, you will see bare wood beneath.

The alternative is to use an oil stain, then follow it with a transparent polyurethane in either gloss or matt finish.

Also becoming more popular are the very attractive preservative stains which both colour and preserve the timber against wood rot and beetle attack. They are very effective, though some of the brighter colours do tend to discolour with weathering if surfaces are not vertical. Available in a limited colour range they offer an excellent alternative to paint for natural wood joinery such as window frames and doors – as long as the joinery is of a high enough standard to stand being seen through the thin coating! Re-treating is very easy, making maintenance of timber-work easy.

If you decide to tackle furniture finishing, you need details of a whole range of finishes from French polish in amateur kit form, to two part cold cure lacquers, oil and wax finishes. This doesn't really come within the scope of simple home maintenance.

Fillers and sealers

This is becoming a very confused area with the introduction of so many materials, but these are the ones you are most likely to encounter.

Powder fillers   Now well established for filling cracks and gaps, you mix an amount of powder with enough water to make a paste. They are fine for cracks in plaster and plasterboard, but are not resistant to damp.

Ready-mixed fillers   There is a move now to supply more fillers ready-mixed in tubs, and this includes what are termed fine surface fillers, or spachtel. These are ideal for filling cracks and gaps in woodwork prior to painting, and when rubbed smooth they give, as the name implies, a very fine surface. Keep well sealed, or they will harden off.

Stopping   This is a good old-fashioned filler with very high adhesion, and it is available in a range of wood colours for jobs where a natural transparent finish will be applied. Note that there is a special external grade for use on exterior woodwork.

Putty   A traditional material which lives on for glazing work, though new mastic materials are creeping in. Remember there are two grades of putty; normal glazing putty, and metal casement putty. The normal grade is used for timber frames, while the metal casement putty is designed to harden in metal frames.

If you use ordinary putty in metal frames, you will find that the linseed oil in the putty won't dry out or be absorbed, so it will remain soft for months. Putty has the disadvantage that it sets hard with age and loses its adhesion – so you don't use it on any surfaces which might move or flex.

Mastic This is a special type of filler which although it hardens on the surface so you can paint it, remains soft and flexible underneath. So this is the type of filler to use where any movement of surfaces is likely, or where a material might shrink slightly. It comes in strip form, rather like Plasticine, in tubes, or in cartridges to be used in a simple mastic 'gun'.

There is a special grade called a bituminous mastic which is ideal for repairs to surfaces like cracked roofing felt. It is much stronger if used with a hessian bandage or glass fibre bandage to add strength to the repair.

Sealant This is really a sophisticated form of mastic based on silicone rubber, and it is available in a range of pastel colours and white, making it ideal for sealing gaps around baths and basins. It has good adhesion, and once set is resistant to water and chemicals. But be warned, it takes practice to get a really nice finish! And you have to push the nozzle forward, not drag it back as you might expect when sealing a gap.

Glazing tape This is a form of bandage covered in a very sticky mastic compound, and it is ideal for sealing gaps out of doors between wood, glass and masonry. There is a type which has aluminium foil on its upper face, and this looks better and is less likely to collect dirt. A typical use would be to seal gaps between the timber bars and sheets of glass on a greenhouse roof – foil face up of course.

This material is also available as a glazing cord, and is ideal for stuffing cracks and gaps. It will seal a gap between lavatory pan and waste pipe where the seal has broken down.

Waterproof tape Another useful repair material is waterproof transparent adhesive tape – not to be confused with the household packaging tape. It can be used for sealing cracks in glass until the glass can be replaced, or sealing gaps and cracks in corrugated plastic roofing sheets. It is unaffected by damp, unlike standard cellophane adhesive tape which will break down when wet.

Cement bandage A relative newcomer, this is a heavy bandage coated in cement. To use, you merely soak the bandage to activate the cement, bind the area to be repaired or sealed, and leave it to set. A very strong joint is formed. Ideal for repairs to damaged gutters and down-pipes, and to corrugated asbestos or iron roofing sheets.

Adhesives

If you are confused over paint types, you will be even more confused by the choice of adhesives. What started out as quite a simple business has become most complex, mainly because of the profusion of man-made materials now used, and in particular because of the development of plastics. The following is designed as a guide, but if you have particular repair or construction problems, you will have to find a store where they have someone who understands adhesives. You will have to take along a sample of material; decide what it is made of; explain what it has to stick to – and let the staff advise you.

Animal glue   This is the familiar glue that many of us grew up with, supplied as a rather smelly liquid either in a tube to be used cold, or in a lump or granules to be melted and used hot. It sticks well, given time to set, but it does tend to be brittle, and it is affected by damp, so it has been replaced by more modern materials in many cases.

Resin powder adhesive   This is mixed with water, but once set it becomes water-resistant, so it is ideal for projects where damp may be encountered. It is slow setting, so it needs the work to be clamped until the glue has set.

PVA adhesive   This is a milky-white liquid, resembling single cream, and it is probably the most versatile adhesive introduced for d-i-y use. It will stick joinery work very effectively, but you will also find it packaged for fixing expanded polystyrene to walls and ceilings, paper and card for school use and certain heavy-weight wallcoverings. It can also be used to make concrete more adhesive, or used as a coating to stop concrete floors dusting.

Clear resin adhesive   This comes in a tube, and is a very sticky, strong smelling adhesive with very good holding properties. On porous surfaces it gives an almost immediate bond, but on impervious surfaces (where nothing will soak in) you do need to coat both surfaces; allow the adhesive to become tacky, then press firmly together. It is best suited to flexible materials as it remains flexible once set – repairs to fabrics, leather and many plastics.

Rubber-based adhesives   You will find two main types here. First the *latex* adhesives where the adhesive is a milky colour with a strongish smell. This is designed for fabric repairs, sealing frayed carpets and similar jobs where there is no great strain. It rubs easily from the fingers.

And secondly there is the *rubber resin* type adhesive with a very strong smell of solvent – which incidentally grips the fingers like a second skin. This is used for sticking down plastic laminates and for repairing any flexible material. As with the clear adhesive, you must allow the adhesive to become touch-dry on impervious materials before you bring your two surfaces together. If you don't, the adhesive doesn't dry out properly and you get a poor bond.

Epoxy resins   These are excellent materials supplied in two smallish tubes, one containing resin, and the other hardener. Nothing happens until you mix equal quantities from each tube together. Then, setting starts by chemical action, and nothing will stop it. There are two main types. One which takes some hours to set hard, and therefore needs the joint holding during setting. And the other is a rapid version which sets in about five minutes – though complete curing takes longer.

The epoxy adhesive is ideal for repairs to metals, glass and pottery. It is not suited to flexible materials as it sets very hard. The only snag is that the repair will have a 'thickness' to it, so you don't want to choose it for repairs to your best cut glass as you will see the join. Choose a special glass repair adhesive in this case.

PVC adhesive   This has been especially formulated to mend items like plastic macs, balls and beach beds made of pvc plastic. You will see it actually softens the pvc, so mind you don't smear it where it is not required as it will leave marks you can't remove. Most other adhesives are no good for pvc as they sit on the surface and seem to stick until dry. Then they can be peeled away quite easily.

Cyanoacrylates   These are the new instant bond materials used first in industry and now on the d-i-y market, in what seems a very small container. One spot on most dense materials, and on natural or artificial rubber, gives an immediate bond which in a matter of minutes is extremely strong. It has the snag that for jobs like broken pottery, where you need time to align all the pieces, it sets before you can put it together. A slower adhesive would be an advantage. And it is not suitable for items which will be washed regularly in hot soapy water, for this dissolves the adhesive.

Take care when using, for it effectively bonds skin to skin! If you do stick your fingers together, don't panic. Merely put some hot soapy water in a bowl; immerse your fingers, allow to soak, then use a spoon handle to prise the fingers apart. No damage will be done.

I think I've said enough to indicate this is a material to keep out of the hands of children!

Rapid bonding system   At the time of writing, a brand new adhesive has been introduced. It is sold as a glass jar of activator and a tube of adhesive. Activator is painted on one surface with the brush supplied, and adhesive is spread on the other surface straight from the tube. Nothing happens until you bring the two together, then setting takes place in seconds, giving a very strong joint. It bonds to metal, glass and most other materials, and it even likes surfaces which are slightly oily. Usually, this is what causes many adhesives to fail to grip – so this really is revolutionary.

Glass adhesive   This is another new material which uses an entirely new approach for bonding. It is a clear material which, if applied by artificial light, will stay liquid. But as soon as the joint is exposed to natural daylight, setting starts. It gives a very strong waterproof joint with no glue line, so you can get really well disguised repairs, though I'm reluctant to use the word 'invisible'.

In addition to these materials, which you will collect for your tool box, you will of course come across adhesives designed for specific jobs. Here again, I would stress that when you buy a decorating material you should ask what is recommended to stick it in place. By far the most failures happen because the wrong adhesive was used – based on a wrong assumption or the desire to use up something left from a previous job.

Wallcovering adhesives The most widely used adhesive now is the cellulose adhesive, because it is easy to mix and it doesn't stain. But remember, it has a high water content, and for heavy papers you would be wise to move to a heavy duty cellulose paste with plenty of 'body' in it. Or, for 'heavyweights', such as Anaglyptas, use what is still called a cold water paste. This, too, is easy to mix, and it is very full-bodied, with plenty of paste to not a lot of water. This gives good adhesion, and it doesn't over-soak the wallcovering.

When using cold water pastes, you still need to size the walls, so you need a *size adhesive*. This rather resembles brown sugar, and it is mixed with water. It adds 'slip' to the wall surface, and adds adhesion to the paste.

In many cases now the wallcovering may be pre-pasted, so your adhesive problems are diminished. But some vinyls still need pasting, and in this case you must buy a vinyl wallcovering adhesive which has a fungicide in it to discourage mould growth.

Other surfaces for which you must use the right adhesive include wall panelling, putting up gypsum coving, fixing ceramic tiles to a wall, fixing ceiling tiles, floor tiles or parquet strip or cork flooring. You must follow the instructions implicitly, both in application, and in removing surplus from other surfaces and yourself! With some of the very sticky materials, ask if you can have some solvent to remove it – or if there is a suitable hand cleaner available.

Tapes In recent years a whole new range of adhesives has been developed with the introduction of special adhesive tapes. These have been available for many years for securing or binding carpets, but now they are available in pad form, double sided, with the strength to hold small accessories such as soap dishes and hooks through to quite large mirrors and mirror tiles.

Obviously, the surfaces to which such items are secured must be strong themselves. You can't stick to poor paint or wall-coverings, as these would fail before the pads. The ideal surface is smooth and hard – like the surface of a ceramic tile.

Wallcoverings

Of course, the most traditional material for walls is wallpaper, but today it is only one of a whole range of materials for decorating. Like most other materials, you get what you pay for, and you will find a very wide quality range. Having said that, it still pays to shop around, for pattern books are revised every two years, and you may well pick up some quality materials which are merely end of range. Do ensure you get all you need at the outset, as there will be little chance of picking up an extra roll later on.

Wallpaper You will see that both paper quality and pattern varies according to price, and if you are a beginner don't be tempted to start with a very cheap material. It may be hard to match, and it will tear easily. Go for a medium priced paper which is strong, with a pattern that needs little or no matching.

As well as standard paper, you will find coated papers designed to withstand wiping though not scrubbing. These are most often used in kitchens and dining rooms. Rarely will you find a washable wallpaper, though they do appear in some Continental pattern books. If you want something that really is washable, you must choose a *vinyl*. You will also find *duplex papers*, where two sheets of paper have been bonded together. These are tougher, and also offer the manufacturer the chance to include texture.

Remember, too, that the heavier the paper the longer it should be allowed to soak before hanging. For really heavy papers, choose a heavy duty paste which has less water content and more 'body'.

One of the heaviest materials is called *Anaglypta*, and this often resembles thin cardboard with a very definite relief pattern. The pattern may be a basket weave, random pattern or plaster daub, while pebbledash is always popular for ceilings.

The advantage of such materials lies in their ability to hide minor irregularities in a wall surface, so they are ideal in older properties where the wall surfaces are not perfect. But do bear in mind they will not repair loose or crumbling walls. Plaster must be repaired and levelled as far as possible before decorating. Also remember that when you hang these papers you need a heavy paste, and you must avoid pressing down the relief pattern at the edges. If you compress the pattern, you will end up with clearly defined lines at the joins.

Anaglyptas can be painted with emulsion, as can the very popular wood chip papers. These are heavy papers with chips of wood trapped between layers, and when painted can look most attractive. Beware cheap imitations where the chips feel very rough to the touch, especially if you have small children who may fall against the wall.

One of the newest 'papers' is an unwoven fabric material which feels far softer than paper and has far more subtle colouring. With this material, the adhesive is applied to the wall, then the paper pressed on to it, making working very easy where space is limited or where you have no pasting table. The only disadvantage is that it tends to scuff easily on exposed external corners, so it is not suitable for areas of 'high traffic'.

Vinyls   The early vinyl wallcoverings were often of poor quality, as printers had not mastered the techniques of printing on plastics. But today printed vinyls can be excellent with the finest of sheens and textures built into the patterns. They are of course more expensive than wallpapers, but they have a far longer life, and are far easier to strip than heavy papers. You merely pull the vinyl away from a backing paper which, if adhering firmly, can be used as a base for the next covering.

In fairness, I should add you can get easy-strip papers too which take away all that hard work so long associated with stripping off a heavyweight paper.

Remember that a vinyl wallcovering needs a special adhesive, and this should contain a fungicide to discourage mould growth. And remember also that it may be more difficult to stick down the seams of a vinyl wallcovering successfully, as it doesn't stick readily to itself. You may have to use a little clear adhesive from a tube once the surface has dried out – especially if you have slight overlaps to deal with.

Many papers and vinyls now come ready-pasted so you need no pasting table. The covering is cut, rolled lightly and laid in a waxed water trough supplied with the paper: this activates the paste. As some walls are more absorbent than others, you may well find that on a dense surface you have more paste than necessary. Don't worry, it can be eased from seams as the covering is pressed into place, then wiped away with a sponge, leaving no marks.

From the beginner's point of view, the advantage of starting with vinyl, is that you will find it so much easier to hang than a standard paper. It can take quite a lot of pulling about, and sticky fingers won't mark the surface.

Introduced recently is a deep textured range of vinyls more resembling floorcoverings – from which I believe they have been copied in many cases. The texture allows for all kinds of relief effects, including tiling, timbers with grain and brickwork with pointing. In fact some very realistic imitations are available which are easy to keep clean and which are cheaper than the real thing.

Imitations play a large part in special effect wallcoverings, and many designs developed for film and television studio sets are now available for home use. Woodgrains, brickwork and stonework, imitation grasscloths and hessians can look most effective in the right settings.

As you move into the upper end of the market, you can of course treat yourself to the authentic wallcovering. Real Japanese grasscloths, cork laid over paint, silks, hessians and woven fabrics are all available – at a price. Remember that most of these materials are not designed to be matched like wallpaper. You will see the seams, and this is accepted. A material which used to be expensive but which now as a result of technological development has come down quite a way, is the flock effect wallcoverings. The type of flock fibre and the method of anchoring has improved so that the surface is not so easily marked or the flock flattened. Even so, they do need care.

Two ancillary products you may come across are *lining paper* and *sheet veneer*. Lining paper is used far less than it used to be, but it still offers a way of smoothing out the minor irregularities of a poor wall surface before hanging a good wallcovering. It is hung horizontally with no overlapping seams, then the wallcovering is laid vertically over it. This method also offers a good foundation if you plan to paper over a previously painted surface, though it is worth a little experimenting first. I have found in many cases that if the paint is sound, clean and well rubbed down, a modern covering will go over it with no more trouble than, perhaps, having a surfeit of paste.

The veneer is of thin expanded polystyrene, and its purpose is to act as an insulator on a cold wall surface, before putting on a wallcovering. In many instances it will greatly reduce, if not cure, condensation on a cold wall surface. If used in an exposed area or in a nursery, it pays to cover the veneer with a vinyl or Anaglypta which is resistant to denting. The veneer is easily damaged unless protected and cats love to scratch it.

Timber

Timber technology is a complex subject so suffice it to say that you will encounter two main types of wood – softwood and hardwood. And the one you will normally use for shelving, simple framing and furniture making will be the softwood. This comes in two forms – rough sawn, which is as it comes off the saw in the mill, and planed all round (par) as it appears after being planed in the mill.

For all simple timber work I would always advise the planed material as it needs little finishing. The main exception is if you are erecting a fence or building a shed frame where it is unnecessary to use planed wood. Remember you pay for the planing!

All timber comes in metric sizes, but you will find that tradition dies hard and many d-i-y shops still mark up as two by one, three by two, or four by four. On close examination you will find these are not exact conversions, but for most jobs it doesn't matter anyway. One very elementary point so often overlooked by amateurs is that a piece of two by two has four times the volume of a piece of one by one. So it costs that much more. Timber can be an extremely strong constructional material, especially when used with a sheet covering, so note that many designs use quite small sections of timber. Amateurs often err on the heavy side unnecessarily, so it costs more and the unit produced is far heavier than it need be.

Hardwoods are used for decorative work – edgings and beadings – and for woodcarving and turning: they are much harder to locate and to buy than softwoods. If you want to learn making furniture in hardwoods, I would strongly advise you to join a suitable evening class to learn the craft. Your joints and your finishes will be on full view, whereas most softwood constructions are hidden by paint or some other decorative finish.

Plywood This is an expensive material to work with, but it is quite easy to cut and to bend in the thinner sections. You will often hear it referred to as three-ply or five-ply, which is the number of sheets sandwiched together with their grains at right angles to make up the sheet thickness.

There are various grades of plywood, from one with a very good quality veneer on each face, through to those which look as if they have been patched. The choice will depend on what you have in mind. If you want a table top which is to be naturally polished, an attractive veneer is required on one surface. If you are making the hidden back of a piece of furniture, then an inferior grade is quite adequate.

There is one more choice – between standard grades suitable for indoor use, and waterproof, for exterior use and for boat building. Any good timber yard will show you the choice of grades and give a guide to price.

Blockboard and laminboard These are excellent materials, but also very expensive for d-i-y work. You will see that the boards consist of an outer veneer of wood with battens sandwiched between. This makes for a very strong material, ideal for making units which have no timber frame or carcase.

Chipboard Here, small chips of wood have been mixed with a bonding material, formed into sheets and allowed to dry to form a quite heavy but very strong board. It is cheaper to use than plywood of the same dimensions, and it is suitable for many furniture construction jobs where the board is to be covered with a veneer or a laminate.

Be warned though: it is not the easiest of materials to cut, and it quickly blunts saw blades. It also pays to buy a good quality board, as some cheaper versions rather resemble a certain type of breakfast food rather than a building board! Also, don't get the board wet, as it may expand considerably, not returning to its former size as it dries.

If you do decide to work in chipboard, it will pay to buy chipboard screws. These are designed to hold better in the board, and are less likely to split it than standard wood screws.

You will also see in the timber yard flooring grade chipboard. This has widely replaced standard tongued and grooved floorboards in modern homes, and it is something worth bearing in mind if you have a timber floor to lay or replace. It gives a smooth, flat surface upon which to lay floorcoverings.

Of the same family is the now well-known veneered chipboard, covered with either a veneer of timber or plastic. It has revolutionised d-i-y furniture, in that it offers board sizes you can't get in natural wood, at a price well below timber prices.

New techniques of construction have to be learned, and special jointing systems, dowelling sets and edge veneers are supplied to help you build units easily and of sufficient strength. Suppliers of these boards also offer books of simple plans, and if you've never worked in veneered chipboard it will pay you to buy a book and follow a design through. My only criticism of the material is that all units do tend to be angular and boxlike. But if you accept this limitation, some very professional units can be constructed very simply.

Hardboard Made of compressed wood fibres, hardboard is an excellent constructional material, cheaper than plywood and very strong. The standard thickness is 3 mm ($\frac{1}{8}$ in), but it is worth remembering that other thicknesses are available including 12 mm ($\frac{1}{2}$ in) and 6 mm ($\frac{1}{4}$ in) – though they may not be so readily available. It comes in two main types; standard, for all internal work, and oil-tempered for exterior work or any location that may be damp.

For decorative work, there is an extensive range of patterned boards and perforated boards, though, again, not every store will stock them.

Remember that it is wise to condition hardboard sheets before they are used, by damping the backs, laying the sheets back to back and leaving for twenty-four hours. This ensures that they don't buckle in use. Also remember that if you want to bend a sheet to a tight curve, you must wet it thoroughly and bend it wet. You cannot do this with oil-tempered board as it cannot absorb water.

For fixing the board you will need deep drive panel pins which sink well into the board so you can hide the nail heads. If used to cover old floorboards where there is a 'spring' in the floor, you may find that panel pins pull out. If this occurs use small ring nails which grip far better. Oil-tempered board makes a very attractive flooring material in its own right – especially if coated with a polyurethane seal. This is ideal if you are setting up home and can't afford parquet. It goes well with rugs and mats, or as a surround to a carpet square.

Plastic laminates You're probably already familar with the virtues of the laminate work top, cutting board or furniture facing. It is attractive, easy to keep clean and long-lasting if not abused. A laminate sheet consists of a backing upon which the patterned paper is laid, then the whole lot is covered with a tough melamine surface. This surface is usually slightly textured or semi-matt so that it doesn't show the scratches or fine cuts imposed by working kitchen tools. A high gloss would show every mark.

Laminate is usually sold by the sheet. As it will cost you extra to have it cut to size, this is another case where it is a good idea to plan units or work tops to come from a set number of sheets. For really small projects like small table tops or place mats, it may pay you to find a store which sells off-cuts of all shapes and sizes. Perhaps you can't be quite so choosy about colour or pattern, but you will keep costs down.

Strips may also be used for lining shelves or covering old window sills; for making splash-backs – or just a protective strip on the back door where a pet always scratches to get out!

Apart from standard pre-formed laminates, there is a special range of what are called post-formed laminates. These can be used to make work tops to order, shaping them at the lip and at the back to give attractive rounded surfaces. This process is also useful for making tops for vanity units into which a basin can be set – so keep this in mind when planning your new kitchen or bathroom.

To stick laminate in place you need a contact or impact adhesive. Ask about this when you buy your laminate.

Self-adhesive plastic sheet Supplied off the roll, the self-adhesive sheeting has been popular over many years. It can be used in a number of ways, including covering small wall areas, decorating old or whitewood furniture or adding decorative panels to decorated furniture. It is available in a wide variety of textures and patterns, including a whole range of effective woodgrains.

The secret of application is to get the material in place without stretching the plastic and without trapping air under the sheet. There is a knack to it, so it is worth practising a little before tackling a finished job. It is best to peel back the backing paper just a little at a time, position the sheet, press in place, then peel off some more. Incidentally I suggest you save the backing papers. They are siliconised, and make excellent work surfaces when working with adhesives, or when positioning laminate over a glued surface.

There is also a range of translucent sheeting in attractive patterns, ideal for giving privacy where clear glass has been used in a window or door. Again, it is most important to make sure you don't trap air between glass and plastic – and of course the glass must be really clean or you will trap dirt where it can't be reached.

If you plan to use woodgrain on furniture, make it look as realistic as possible by ensuring that the grain runs the longest lengths. And make as few joins as possible as they can be hard to lose.

There are many other materials you will encounter, but one grouping that comes to mind is that of tiles. The tile has become very popular because it is very easy to handle, simplifies fixing and cutting, and is easily transported. It is only fair to say that I think there has been a move back to sheet materials in floor-covering as the patterns can be more imaginative, and you can get an unbroken effect now room-width sheets have been introduced. Even so, there will always be a market for good tiles.

There are vinyl floor tiles, carpet squares, expanded poly-styrene ceiling tiles, mirror tiles, cork wall and floor tiles and parquet floor tiles. All need their correct methods of fixing, so be sure to ask when you buy.

As you become more experienced, you may well venture into projects which require building materials such as cement, sand, bricks, blocks or paving slabs. Here, you will find the Building Centres useful, and if you have one near you, pay a visit to its free exhibition.

Many of the garden centres also cater for materials likely to be used in garden work, and you can also learn a lot from a visit to a good builders' yard. Remember that most of these materials are very heavy – though they may not seem so when the experts are moving them about.

Before embarking on adventurous projects like paving or laying concrete, do seek advice. You may well realise that certain jobs are best left to the professional. Or there may be ways around the problem like having concrete delivered ready-mixed to the site, or using smaller sizes of slab, or working in blocks which a child can handle individually.

3

Jobs about the house

The jobs to be done about the house are varied, but for simplicity I have tried to group them under main headings. Each basic operation has its own section so you can study them separately – or read through the lot in one go. With any of these jobs, practice makes perfect, so don't be afraid to experiment. But when you have found a material or method which gets good results – stick to it! You can waste a lot of time and money for ever experimenting with things the adverts tell you are a 'must' for success.

Decorating

It has always been said that about ninety per cent of the job is in the preparation, and despite all the developments in recent years, this is still true. If the surfaces are not clean, dry and 'keyed' to take a new material, you will end up with very poor results.

Stripping

As a general rule, don't strip paint unless it is flaking away or breaking up. All that may be required is a rub over with a damp stripping block to remove surface dirt (*Figure 10*), rub down the

Figure 10

glossy surface and give a good key for a new coat of paint. But if the paint is damaged, it must come off.

You have a choice of methods, but the safest for a beginner is the chemical stripper. Protect your eyes and all exposed areas of skin and keep children and pets away, then apply the stripper to the paint, laying it on thick rather than brushing it out. You will see the paint start to bubble and blister, but don't be hasty. Leave it until there are signs that the stripper is starting to dry out, then use a scraper or shave hook to scrape the paint away (*Figure 10*).

If the paint was thin, one coat may take you down to bare wood. But if there were many coats, you may need two or three applications before the wood comes clean. The point of a shave hook will get in (most) corners, but wire wool is useful for cleaning mouldings and decoration (*Figure 11*). When the

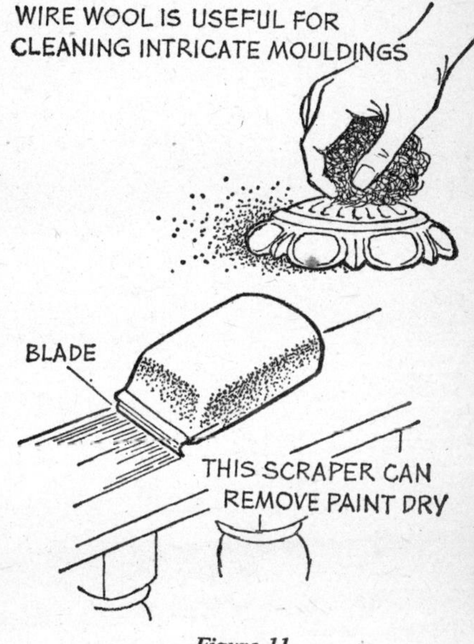

Figure 11

paint is off, be sure to read the instructions on the can or bottle as to how the stripper is neutralised before finally wiping down. And take sensible precautions when storing or disposing of the container.

An alternative method is to clean off areas with a special scraper (*Figure 11*). This has a surgically sharp blade specially shaped so that it will scrape paint off down to bare wood. It works best on slightly convex surfaces, but be careful, for you can tear too much wood away. This tool can save you quite a bit of chemical stripper on items like chairs and banister rails. It is not so easy to use on flat panels such as doors.

The third way is to use a bottle gas blowtorch with a spreader on the end, but be warned, it does need practice. You have to make sure you don't burn the wood, by keeping the torch moving

Figure 12

at all times. You must keep the flame off your hand – and make sure no burning paint drops on your hand – or on to any surface which could be spoiled (*Figure 12*). And you must keep the flame off surrounding surfaces such as window glass, or wall-covering you don't want to remove.

It is best to use it first on an item like a kitchen chair where you can take it well away and practice. Once you get the hang of it, it is a fast and relatively cheap way of stripping.

Never, ever work with curtains in place, with newspaper on a floor or near any material which will burn. Take extreme care in bright sunlight, as you won't be able to see the flame at all at times.

It is wise to keep a bucket of water near the job, and if paint comes away still burning, drop it in the bucket.

Whatever method you have used, when the paint is off, you need to smooth down the wood with fine glasspaper. This removes traces of remaining burned paint, and any slight charring of the wood if a blowtorch was used. Remember always to rub only with the wood grain – never across it. Scratches across the grain are difficult, if not impossible, to remove. Smoothing will also take down any raised grain caused by the wetting effects of chemical stripper, and it is worth spending a long time on this operation as the new finish depends upon it.

Stripping paper is another job you will probably have to tackle. If a thin wallpaper was used, this may not be too hard a job. You merely wet the paper with water on a sponge or paint roller; allow it to soak, then scrape it away with a wide-bladed scraper. If it won't move, wet it some more. Don't dig the scraper into the plaster. If a thicker paper was used, it may help to make up a mix of cellulose paste, washing up liquid and water (*Figure 13*). The paste holds the water against the paper, while the washing up liquid acts as a wetting agent.

If the paper is washable or wipeable, you will have to score the surface with a pan scourer or an everlasting sanding block (a metal plate with pieces of abrasive fused to it) (*Figure 13*). This will allow the water to soak through to the paste. Don't use wire wool, for my experience is that tiny fragments get embedded in the plaster, where they rust and can cause stains on new coverings.

If the covering just won't move, hire a steam wallpaper stripper from your local hire shop. The steam from the face plate will soften the adhesive behind the toughest paper, and you will be able to pull it off by the sheet.

If you are lucky enough to have a wall covered in easy-strip paper or vinyl wallcovering, the job is easy. Merely lift up a corner and pull. The whole top sheet will come away, leaving

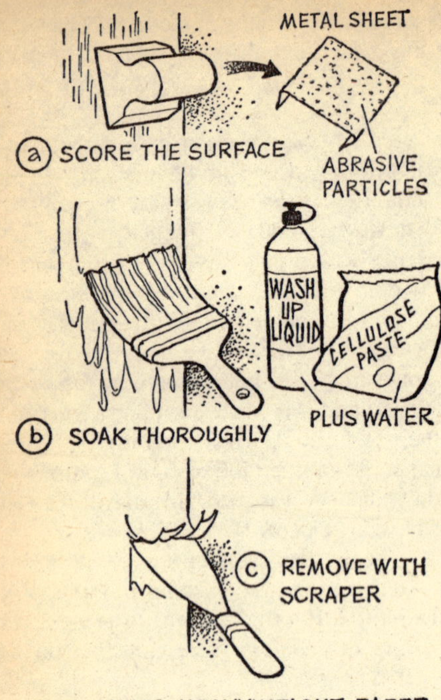

Figure 13

a backing paper behind. If the backing is firmly in place and not bubbling, it can be used as the lining paper for the next covering to go on.

I am often asked if you can decorate over an existing paper. While always frowned upon by manufacturers, it is possible to go over a paper which is firmly adhering to a wall with a new material assuming you have a smooth paper and not a textured surface – but there is always the danger that the new paste will loosen the old and allow blistering. A little experimenting is called for. If a covering is grubby or greasy – take it off.

The same applies to painting over wallpaper. You may well get away with it, but experimenting is advisable to see if the paper bubbles up, and if it does, whether the bubbles go when the paint dries out. Materials like Anaglyptas are no problem. You can repaint with little fear of trouble unless too weak an adhesive was used initially. Wood chips can also be painted. Vinyls can only be painted with a vinyl-based paint – but be prepared for the texture in the vinyl to 'grin' through at you.

Figure 14

To strip ceiling paper use the same method as for a heavy wallpaper — though you have to defy gravity to get water on the ceiling! One simple way of getting the water there is to use a garden spray filled with warm water and a little liquid detergent (*Figure 14*).

Expanded polystyrene ceiling tiles are hard to remove as you so often get left with lumps of adhesive on the ceiling. Often this can be removed by heating a scraper blade so the heat softens the adhesive, but it doesn't always work. If the tiles are very well stuck, and you can see adhesive was used all over as it should be to meet fire precautions, consider putting new tiles over the old. You will lower the ceiling a fraction – but you will get even better insulation value from it. Remember if you want to paint ceiling tiles, the ideal time to do them is before you stick them up! Never paint them with gloss paint, as this could be a fire risk.

Vinyl floor tiles are also difficult to remove because of the tough adhesive used. One of the most effective ways I have found is to lay kitchen foil over a tile then apply a hot domestic iron (*Figure 15*). This softens the vinyl, making it easier to pull

Figure 15

away. You can then use a heated scraper to remove any residue of adhesive.

Filling

Once all your surfaces are clean, there are sure to be numerous holes, cracks and gaps to fill. A cellulose filler is fine for plaster walls. Take it proud of the surface, leave it to set, then rub it flat with a piece of glasspaper wrapped around a wood block. For holes in woodwork, use a fine surface filler or one of the pre-mixed fillers recommended for the job. If the wood is outside, use an exterior grade filler, or what is called a wood stopping, waterproof grade. As with the wall repairs, take your material above the level required, then rub it back with glasspaper.

Remember to use a fine grade glasspaper or you will make unnecessary scratches on the filler surface. Where a largish hole has been filled, rubbing the blade of a wide-bladed scraper over the repair is a good way of getting the filler dead level with the surrounding material.

Remember that fillers only adhere to sound materials. They won't grip to crumbling plaster or rotting timber. You must always cut back to sound material, remove all dust or debris with an old paintbrush kept for the job, then apply the new filler.

Gaps around window and door frames should be filled with a mastic rather than a filler which sets hard. The mastic remains flexible even when set, so any slight movement in the fabric will not cause a fracture of the seal. If you encounter cement or putty seals which are cracking, dig them out and reseal with mastic.

Painting

When decorating, your painting jobs will fall into two main categories, each with its own techniques. First, there is the joinery – doors, windows, skirtings, rails, staircase. And secondly, there are the walls and ceilings. Let us look at each in turn.

Painting woodwork and metalwork will involve the same basic rules, and as with most things it is a case of practice makes perfect. Choose the best quality brush for the job, and use the one which has a width suitable to the job in hand – narrow 12 mm ($\frac{1}{2}$ in) for window bars, mouldings and rails; wider 25 mm (1 in) or 37 mm ($1\frac{1}{2}$ in) for panels and wider strips; wide 100 mm (4 in) or 125 mm (5 in) for flush doors. Remember modern paints dry quickly, and it can be difficult to keep what is called a 'wet edge' to the paint if you are taking ages covering an area with small brush strokes.

Make sure the surface you plan to paint is clean, dry, smooth and dust and grease free. You can paint over most old paint, but you must rub it down with what is called a pumice stripping block. This takes the glaze off the paint and offers a good key for the next coat. If there is to be a drastic change of colour, you must use an undercoat to obliterate the old colour before you put on a new top coat which has no obliterating power. And if there is any bare wood or metal, it must be treated with a suitable primer. This is most important with wood, otherwise your new paint will merely soak into the grain of the wood, however much you apply. Use a primer on metal to prevent rusting or corrosion.

Choose a good quality fresh paint, and read the instructions about stirring. If it says don't it implies it is a jelly paint which needs no mixing and which will thin if stirred. But if it is a standard gloss it usually says stir well to get all the ingredients which have separated well mixed up. If you have a large can, decant some into a paint kettle, or for small areas perhaps a jam jar.

Actual application will vary according to the type of paint, and here too it is wise to practise. A thixotropic, or jelly paint, is laid on and smoothed rather than brushed out so you get quite a thick layer. A normal gloss, which is quite thin, is brushed out, for if you apply it too thickly it will merely drip, form runs or sag into 'curtains'.

Always work with the strokes ending along the length of the piece being painted; that usually means along the grain of wood. You can use strokes in other directions as you apply the paint, but the final strokes are the crucial ones – along the length. If further coats have to be applied, make sure the previous coat is completely dry. A guide to drying time should be given on the can. If you hurry the job, it is possible for the new coat to soften up the under-coat and you will get marks which cannot be smoothed away.

If you should get slight bits, or nibs, in the surface of a coating, once it is really hard, give it a light rub down with a very fine grade of glasspaper to remove the bits. Then use a 'tack' or 'tacky rag' to collect up the dust – this is a duster treated with a special non-setting resin to which dust will stick, and it is an ideal way of getting a surface really clean once it has been dusted off with a brush.

If little flies get stuck in your painted surface while the paint is drying, leave them there! Then, when the paint is hard you will find you can rub most of the debris away. Lifting them from wet paint will make a bigger mess. This leads to the point that

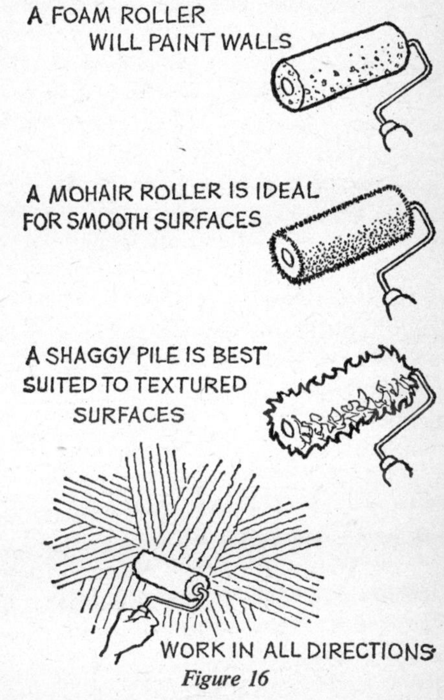

Figure 16

outside work is best done on calm days, and ideally at a time of year when the air isn't full of insects and fine dust.

Remember also when painting outside not to leave bare metal or wood for any length of time as, untreated, it may deteriorate. Plan your work in small enough sections to be able to at least get primer and undercoat in place. Paint openable windows and doors as early in the day as possible if you have to close them overnight.

For wall painting, while a wide brush is still an acceptable tool to use, there are alternatives. You can use a paint roller or a paint pad.

There are three main types of paint rollers (*Figure 16*). First, the foam sleeve roller for general painting. Be careful of spatter, and don't compress the roller while in use or it will drip paint. It has the advantage that the sleeve is removable for cleaning. Then there is the mohair roller, which has a very fine pile on a quite hard base. This is ideal for large smooth areas, and it gives a very fine finish. Because it has a short pile, only a small amount of paint is applied, so it may be necessary to build coat on coat to get a really solid colour. The sleeve is not removable, so cleaning needs care and thoroughness if the mohair is to remain soft. Finally there is the shaggy pile roller in nylon or

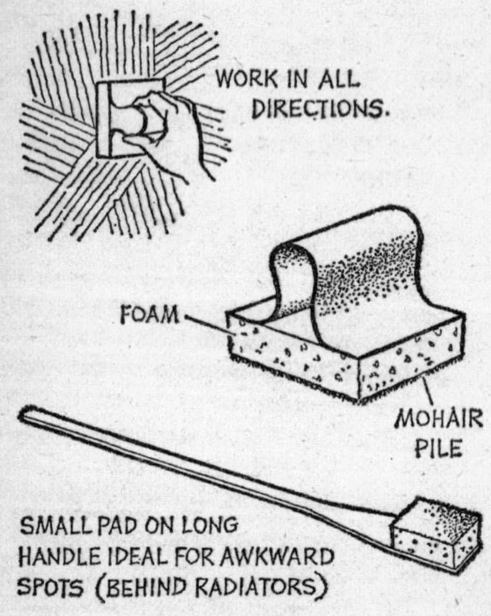

Figure 17

wool which is best suited to textured or relief surfaces. The shaggy coating gets into all the nooks and crannies. You will find that there are specially tough exterior grade rollers, and these can be used on textured renderings with certain masonry paints. Cleaning is again a problem as you must get the pile clear of all old paint if it is to remain soft and pliable.

Because of the cleaning problems, it is wise to use water-based paints with rollers and pads as they are so much easier to clean in water. And many of the brush cleaning fluids necessary with a standard oil-based paint can attack the adhesive used to fix certain piles in place.

A paint pad consists of a mohair pad bonded to a foam backing, which in turn is fixed to some form of grip or handle (*Figure 17*). It resembles no previous painting tool – which has discouraged some painters from trying it. But in use it can apply a coating very easily, with little splashing or dripping – and is far faster than a brush.

A standard brush is used in a fairly regular pattern (*Figure 18*), always finishing off in one direction. But you will see in Figures 16 and 17 that a roller or pad brush can be used in any random pattern in any direction, as long as you make sure that the surface has been covered adequately. Thin coats are better than thick ones, and as water-based paint dries quickly, plan to apply two or perhaps three coats rather than one thick one. This also ensures that any small areas you missed – particularly on textured surfaces – will be covered by following coats.

You may find that the pad or roller doesn't reach close to ceilings and in corners, so have a small paintbrush handy just to finish off these spots. You may note that certain rollers and pads have hollow handles designed to take a broom handle so that you can reach high areas from ground level. This sounds appealing, but my experience is that you can't beat getting close to a job if at all possible. If you are disabled or elderly, this extension may give you the chance to decorate areas you otherwise couldn't reach which is fine. But I think you must accept it won't be as perfect a job as you could otherwise get.

One accessory I have not mentioned which does prove useful is a paint tray. For a roller it is wise to use one with an area where the roller can be rolled up and down to even up the paint loading. But for pads, a flat baking tray is fine. Pads only need dipping on the paint surface to load them.

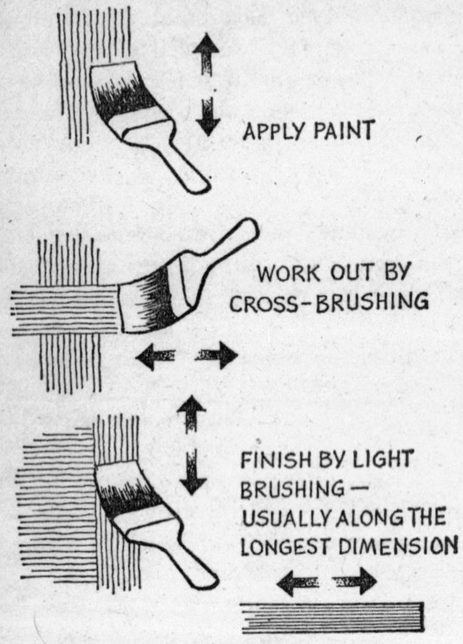

Figure 18

Papering walls

Good wallpaper shops now offer you illustrated leaflets which clearly demonstrate how to hang wallpaper, so I think the space here is far better used offering tips which come from experience, and which you rarely find on leaflets.

Remember to clear a room as far as possible of furniture and fittings, and cover anything not removable with dust sheets in the centre of the room. Then make sure you have a firm pair of kitchen steps so you can reach the highest point to be papered.

Now take a roll of wallcovering and measure it against the wall, cutting a length so you have 50 mm (2 in) to spare at each end.

Now re-measure the roll against the wall and note how much you would have to cut off to get a match for your first piece. If it is considerably more than you need for trimming, put that roll aside and try another roll, picking one with little waste. By alternating rolls, you will often find you will save on each length – and in a fair-sized room this can amount to a full length.

If the pattern is large, decide where you want it to be cut at picture rail level. It can affect the final appearance. If the height of the room varies, try not to pick up a part of the pattern which will accentuate the error. The same of course applies to verticals. It is very easy to highlight errors in the room when the eye has a pattern to judge them against.

When you paste your first length, be sure to work from the centre out (*Figure 19*). In this way you ensure that no paste is

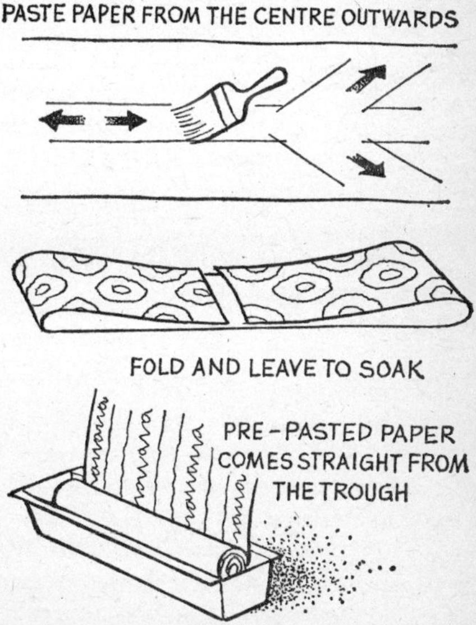

Figure 19

pushed under the edges by the brush. And if the paper is heavy, leave it to soak while you paste a second length. This will give it time to expand fully – and you will avoid blisters and bubbles. If you've folded it paste to paste, the paper won't dry out during this waiting time.

If you have chosen a pre-pasted paper, where you pull it straight from a water trough on to the wall, this problem of expansion has been allowed for, and there is no need to put the length to soak. If you follow the recommendations concerning time in the trough, plus a few seconds to drain off the surplus water, all will be well.

The same applies to vinyls. These don't expand like the papers, so there is little danger of blistering. The most common cause of bubbles occurs when pasting unpasted lengths and areas are missed. You will feel these with your fingers through the vinyl as 'dry' areas. If it is too late to pull the length away and put some paste on the wall, you will have to slit the vinyl with a razor blade and slip some paste in on a fine camel hair brush, or use a hypodermic syringe loaded with paste.

When trimming papers, crease the paper into the skirting board or picture rail with the back of your decorating scissors. then pull the paper away and trim 3 mm ($\frac{1}{8}$ in) to the waste side, This will give you a little flap which hides any crack between wall and skirting board. This also applies at windows and doors. I would always use scissors to cut wet paper, for however sharp a craft knife, it will tend to rip rather than cut cleanly. Vinyl is different for it has a rigid surface even when the paper backing is wet, so you may find trimming with a craft knife and straight-edge gives you a neater edge.

For cutting round switches and fittings, a pair of nail scissors will be easier to handle and make neater cuts. But if a switch or fitting can be loosened to give a small gap, you will get a neater effect by tucking a millimetre or two of paper behind it. Never use a metal implement to push the paper in unless the current has been switched off at the mains. An iced lolly stick makes a good implement.

If you find you run short of paper plan to use the left-overs where it won't show – around radiators and behind wall units.

You should always start work at feature areas. The chimney breast is a crucial area, especially if you have an open fire, so decide where your key piece will go on the projecting wall. It may be central if you get a neat turn around the edges, or it may look better with two pieces meeting down the centre line. You will have to be guided by the pattern, and the width of the wall at this point.

Always try to turn at least 75 mm (3 in) around an external corner, especially if the wall is not too true. If the turn flap is out top to bottom, don't butt the next piece to the error, but take a new vertical and, where necessary, overlap the paper.

Where there is a bulge in a wall and the paper won't lie flat but wants to crease, learn to be quite ruthless, and tear the paper along the line of the crease. (*Note*: a tear shows less than a straight cut.) Now smooth the paper back in place, making sure that any protruding paper fibres behind the pattern are on the under-piece. The overlap will then lie nice and smoothly in place with little or no sign of the tear.

Another point to bear in mind is that at some point in the room, the pattern won't match that coming from the opposite direction. Again, you can work this mis-match so that it occurs at a point least noticed – over a curtained window, or behind a fixed wall unit. It is these little points which, if ignored, become a worry when you are finishing off.

Finally, do remember that if you have a relief material you must not press the paper down at the seams. If you do, you will have visible 'tram lines' at the joints. Of course, you must make sure it is adhering to the wall, but apply a minimum of pressure.

Papering ceilings

Remember you have an enemy here, working against you – force of gravity, releasing your paper as fast as you press it home. So the secret is to use a really heavy paste plus a glue size on the ceiling to increase adhesion. And be sure to allow the paper plenty of time to soak. Bubbles on the ceiling tend to show up very clearly when illuminated. If you fold the paper concertina-style so paste is to paste, the paper won't dry out. Then be sure you have a good working platform which puts your head within about 75 mm (3 in) of the ceiling – closer and you will get a crick in your neck; further away and you will get arm-ache. An assistant will be a great help who, with a soft broom, can hold the start of your length to the ceiling until you get enough up there to make it stay unsupported (*Figure 20*). Again,

Figure 20

if you are working with an Anaglypta with high relief, don't press the pattern down too hard or you will get visible lines at the joins. A soft paint roller is a good tool to bed the paper as it is firm enough yet yielding.

If you have to cut around ceiling roses, make some careful measurements and cut at least a small star before you paste through which you can pull the flex and lampholder. This is a very tricky job to perform if left until you put the paper up, as you will find you haven't enough hands!

Always work from the window, away. The reason for this is that should you get any overlaps, light will be reflected off the paper edge, effectively hiding them. If you work the other way, you will throw a tiny shadow off the edge which cannot be hidden.

As with wallpapers, decorating scissors are best for marking and trimming. A craft knife will tend to rip rather than cut wet paper.

Coving

You will find there are two main types of coving – expanded polystyrene and gypsum plaster. The expanded polystyrene is by far the simplest to fix as it is light. And it comes in short, easy to handle lengths. Because it isn't very strong, it is best to put it up as a last finishing touch, rather than try to paper up to it. But do bear in mind that you won't be able to disguise joints. You must learn to live with them. Don't try rubbing down edges with glasspaper; you will just rough up the plastic. At best you can use a new razor blade to pare down a protruding edge, but even this is fraught with problems.

You can buy systems with ready-made internal and external angles, but don't try to force these to conform with irregular or inaccurate corners. Let the polystyrene find its own correct position, then fill in any gaps with a filler. Wipe off surplus before it sets, as you can't rub it down with glasspaper afterwards.

Plaster coving is an entirely different proposition. It can be bought in long pieces so you need no joints. It looks far more professional, and it gives a good hard edge up to which you can decorate. Internal and external angles are not easy to cut even though the material is quite soft, as, mechanically, it does need some care to produce a matching angle. If you can practise on a spare piece, do, using the template provided with the coving.

Fixing is incredibly easy, using a special plaster-based adhesive. No nails or pins are required, but you will need an extra pair of hands while you lift your length in place and press it to the ceiling and wall. Full instructions are supplied with the coving, concerning preparing the ceiling and wall, and filling any minor gaps you may end up with.

The most important point is to let the coving find its own level on irregular walls. You cannot force it to follow undulations in the surface. Any small gaps can easily be filled in later with some of the plaster adhesive, as can any gaps at the corners.

The coving is now supplied in short lengths which, obviously, are easier to handle and fix. But you do come back to this problem of hiding the joints. It is easier than with expanded polystyrene, but don't expect such perfect results as with one clean run where a length goes wall to wall.

As well as looking decorative, a coving offers the ideal way of hiding a crack between wall and ceiling. This is always a weak spot in a house, and you can very rarely hide these cracks with filler for very long. A coving will 'lose' them for ever.

Tiling walls

Again, I won't devote space going through the basic tiling process. You will find it very well described and illustrated on any tiling leaflet. I would rather give some general hints and tips.

First, remember that modern thin ceramic tiles can be stuck over any firm, clean surface, with few exceptions. You can stick over old tiles, glass, hardboard and of course plaster. You cannot stick over wallpaper: It must come off. And if a wall is painted, you must key the surface by scratching with an abrasive pad, otherwise the weight of tile could pull the paint off.

So, if you have the old 6 in square glazed tiles so popular in the twenties and thirties, don't try to chip them off; tile over them. There will be a problem though, if you are changing from half-tiling to floor-to-ceiling tiling, for there will be a ledge to lose, or to accentuate. (*Figure 21* shows three approaches to the problem.)

The crucial factor when tiling is that you must start from a truly horizontal line. Don't rely on the floor, or on the line of a basin or bath. You must use a spirit level and a good straight edge to give you a working line one tile above floor or ledge, then everything else will fall into place.

The biggest headache in tiling is deciding what pattern, if any, you want; how many tiles of each colour, and how many edge tiles. You will see that the edge ones have no little nibs or spacers, so you get a neater finish. But research is in progress designed to simplify the whole system, so keep your eyes open for any announcements suggesting one tile which will do both jobs – main and edge tiling. When ordering, allow for ten per cent wastage. That will allow for accidental breakages, plus trimming and fitting.

THREE WAYS OF DEALING WITH A LEDGE

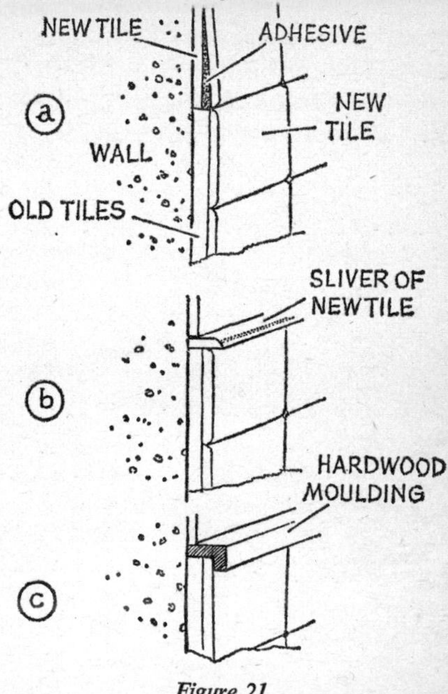

Figure 21

If you plan to do a lot of tiling, invest in a good tile cutter. This may be a wheel device which you pull across a tile, or a little platform with a wheel set in it, over which you push a tile. And there is a new pliers-action cutter which, having scored the tile, will break it neatly for you with just a little hand pressure. Any tile shop will explain these tools to you.

Cutting a tile is very easy – as long as the cutting wheel scores the glaze cleanly, the tile will snap along the line. A simple way is to lay the tile over two match sticks lined up with the score, and just press either side. It does get a little more tricky when you have fine strips to cut off, and a piece of wood with a slot will help.

Shaping tiles is best done with a little tool called a tile file –

which is just what its name suggests (*Figure 22*). This can be used in a fretsaw frame, or there is a version with a handle of its own. The file will cut curves or remove fine slivers in a way you would never achieve with a tile cutter.

I find the grouting is best applied with a small piece of sponge, pressing it well between tiles. Wipe off the surplus, but don't

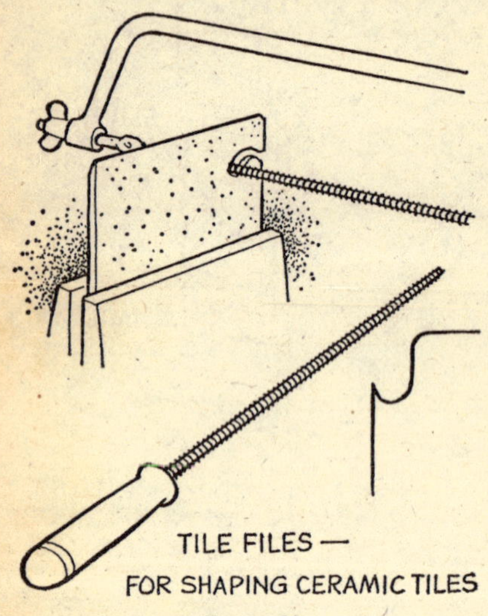

Figure 22

worry too much at this stage if the whole job looks a mess. Once dry, screw up a double page of newspaper and use it to scrub off the surplus grouting. You will be amazed how the tiling is transformed. Why newspaper? I've no idea, except that nothing does the job better, or leaves a nicer shine!

Painting the ceiling

You can look upon the ceiling as a rather difficult wall. The painting technique will be the same, but you have gravity to contend with! For a smooth ceiling, a mohair paint roller is best for applying emulsion paint; or use a large pad brush.

Work close to the ceiling, as recommended for papering (p.62), and if you have the choice, work in daylight, as you can see where you have been far more clearly. If this is impossible, put on one coat at night and a second coat in daylight.

Never overload a roller or brush, or you will have paint running down your arm and dripping on the floor. It is far better to apply two or three thin coats. Don't work in a heated room, for the hottest part will be at ceiling level, any you may find the emulsion drying too quickly, giving a patchy finish.

If you have a textured ceiling, use a shaggy pile roller which will get in the crevices. A pad brush will work too, but you will almost certainly need more than one coat. The second coat always has the advantage of filling crevices missed by the first coat.

Coating existing ceiling tiles isn't easy, and you may need a combination of roller or pad, and a small paint brush to line in between tiles. If you are applying new ceiling tiles, paint them before you put them up: it is far easier. Remember that ceiling tiles must be given an over-all coating of adhesive, and not the old five blob method which encourages a fire as the tiles tend to drop away from the adhesive blobs. Tiles stuck all over are safe providing you don't use an oil-based (gloss) paint. Use an emulsion paint or a fire retardant paint.

Floors

The most important thing to ensure when decorating floors is that the floor is dry and smooth. The quickest way to wear out carpet or vinyl is to lay them on a rough or irregular floor. Similarly, damp will rot most woven materials, or at least make them smell musty. Under vinyl, although it won't affect the floorcovering itself, the trapped moisture will cause rot in a timber floor (*see* section on damp p. 85).

A concrete floor should be smooth, but this is not always the case, even in new homes. Small projections in the concrete can be chipped away with a steel chisel and club hammer – but be sure to protect your eyes with safety goggles. But where a floor is uneven, the simplest way to smooth it is to lay a cement-based screeding compound (*Figure 23*). You will get this at a builders' merchants as a dry powder to which you add water according to the instructions. Then it is merely tipped out, spread with an old broom, and left to set. It spreads rather like syrup, so is self-levelling, eliminating the need for trowelling, which really is a job for the professional. Once set, you can put your new decoration over the top

Figure 23

The same material can be used for levelling old flagstones or floor tiles, providing the floor is clean and dry before you start.

With timber floors, you need to punch down all protruding floor nails and remove any small pins or tacks. This is vital if you plan to level the floorboards using a floor sanding machine. The machine offers a quick way of providing a smooth surface, and your hire shop will advise you which grades of abrasive to use.

It depends whether you are moving a lot of wood, or just giving the floor a smooth over.

Another way of tackling a sound but undulating floor is to cover the boards with hardboard. It pays to lay paper between boards and hardboard, as the rubbing between the two can cause groaning noises. Deep drive pins can be used for fixing, but if you find the floor springs enough to loosen the pins, use small ring nails, which get a far better grip. One point to bear in mind is access to pipes or cables under the floor. If you need to get at certain areas, it pays to have sections of board held with screws instead of nails.

If the floor is in bad condition, it may be necessary to get someone to replace the boards. Flooring grade chipboard is a good alternative to floorboards. It is easier to lay and gives a much smoother surface.

With the floor prepared, remember most floorcoverings benefit from some form of underlay; it feels kinder to the feet, has some degree of insulation, and you will get less wear on the top decorative surface. With vinyls, there are now cushioned varieties which have an integral foam backing. And with carpeting, you have the choice of foam-backed carpet, or a standard woven carpet with a good quality underlay beneath. This may be the traditional felt or a more modern textured or dimpled foam underlay. A special double sided tape is a good way to keep the underlay in place, otherwise it is easy to ruckle it when laying carpet.

Wall to wall carpet needs anchoring in place, otherwise furniture will ruckle it when moved. When buying carpet, ask about anchor strips. Types are available for foam-backs and standard carpets – but you may feel this is a job best left to an expert. Look for companies offering a free fitting service.

Furniture

Restoring old pieces of furniture can be a very pleasant and rewarding pastime. Very often, stripping down and repainting can give a new lease of life to jaded pieces. A word of warning here – we are not talking about antiques. Before you take on the task of restoring valuable pieces of furniture you need to do a lot of reading and even more practising. One of the best places would be a good evening class where you can be taught how to restore. Without such tuition you could ruin valuable items perhaps causing irreparable damage.

A chemical stripper is the best method of removing old finishes, and you will find a number about which are recommended for such work. The secret is to be patient and allow the chemicals to do their work before any stripping is done. And you may need more than one coat to get it all off. The same tools can be used as for stripping windows and doors – a shave hook, stripping knife for flat surfaces, a cabinet scraper, and wire wool for getting into cracks and crevices.

Remember always to work with the grain of the wood to avoid scratches across the grain. And be gentle with your scrapers or you may take slivers of wood away with the paint or varnish. It is possible to use a power sander in places, but they can be rather fierce in action, and varnishes can clog up abrasive pads or discs because of the heat generated. Special open coat abrasives are available – mounted on a fine mesh – which don't clog so easily (*Figure 24*).

If you have experience with a blowtorch, it will be a cheaper way of stripping wood, but you must take care not to scorch the wood. Keep the torch on the move all the time, and bring it away from the job while scraping. Usual safety precautions apply (*see* p. 49).

With all the finish off, you may find a wood stain underneath which you would like to remove too. This can be done with what is called a wood bleach, obtainable from good hardware and decorating shops. But do read the instructions concerning care and safety.

The wood will probably be rough after cleaning, so work at it with fine glasspaper, working only with the grain of the wood. Keep at it until the wood feels silky smooth, then dust it off thoroughly. You can now restain, varnish or paint, as you wish.

I am often asked about items for the nursery. What is a really safe paint to use on furniture? The answer is an enamel. You will find the company which does small tins for modelling also sells small tins for whitewood painting. As long as the wood is clean and smooth you need no primer or undercoat – just a smooth coat of enamel. Apply it thinly and build up two or three coats, and you will have a superb gloss finish which is completely harmless even if chewed.

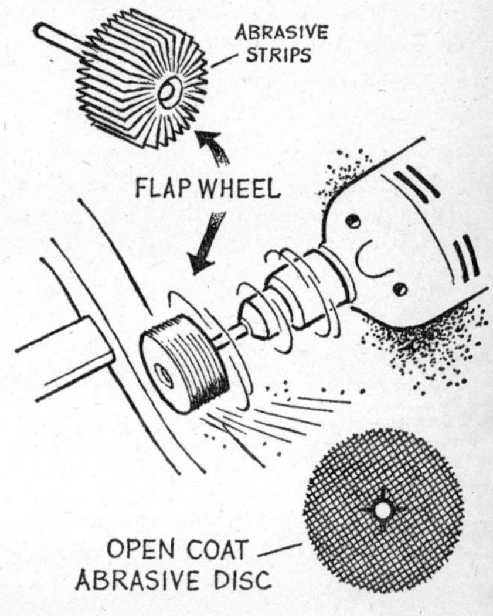

REMOVING AN OLD FINISH

Figure 24

Very often you will find items such as chairs have loose joints, caused by a combination of wood drying out, deterioration of the glue and a lot of use or abuse. If you encounter this, use a rubber hammer or mallet to knock the joints apart (*Figure 25*). Never use a metal hammer or you will bruise the wood. Clean off all old glue with an old chisel and wood rasp, then apply a modern adhesive, such as a pva woodworking adhesive, and reassemble.

To hold the parts together while setting, use strips of old

cycle inner tube rather like large rubber bands (*Figure 25*). This is elastic and will apply a steady pressure without bruising the wood. Small parts may be held by G clamps, but protect the wood with scrap pieces of softwood.

Where you encounter items like broken rails, again dismantle the piece of furniture, repair the rail, then reassemble.

Figure 25

You can also transform a piece of furniture by removing the old fitting and replacing with new, keeping within the style of your piece. Check to see how knobs and pulls are secured (*Figure 26*). Obviously, it will be easiest to fit new ones in the same way as the old – but failing that you may have to do some plugging of holes with pieces of matching wood glued in place then smoothed before the new hardware is applied.

To repair chairs with damaged seats, carefully dismantle the seat covering to see where the damage lies. It may be a splintered plywood seat which needs replacing, or it may be that the webbing has failed. You will find the necessary repair materials at your local upholstery shop. And for webbing you may find the modern rubber webbing and clips a good way of effecting a repair. Ask for a leaflet explaining how to fix and tension the webbing.

For more complicated upholstery jobs, you will have to get a book on the subject. And again if you can find an evening class with an expert teacher, this is the ideal way of both learning and getting the job done properly.

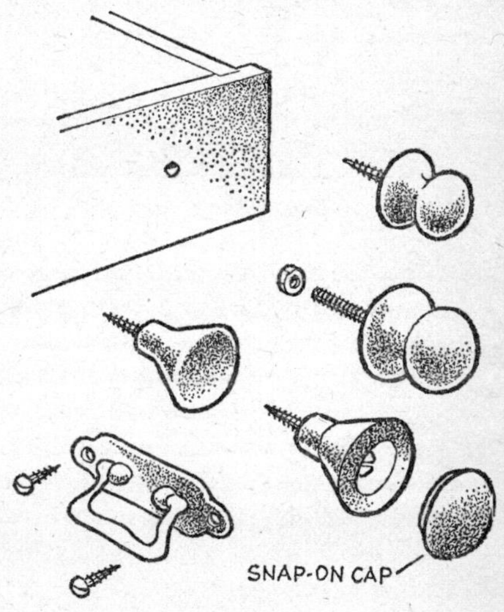

FIXING METHODS FOR HANDLES

Figure 26

Cupboards

Remember when fixing cupboards to a wall, the screws must go through to firm masonry (*Figure 27*). You cannot fix into the thickness of the plaster. See what is the largest screw you can get through any fixing plates; choose a masonry drill to suit the screw size and a plug to suit the drill. Be sure to use a spirit level to ensure that the cupboard is truly horizontal.

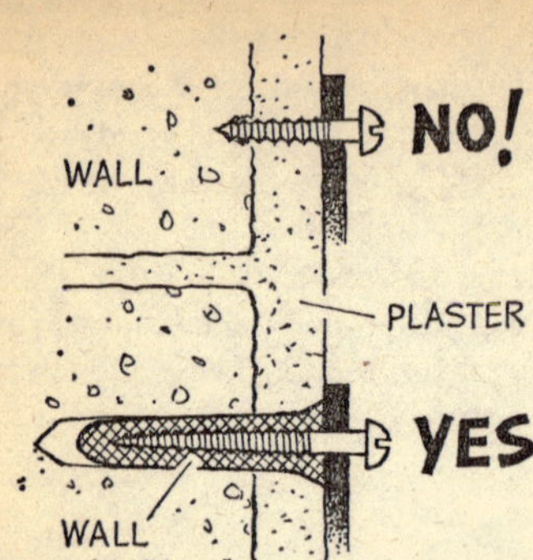

Figure 27

If the cupboard has to carry a lot of weight, it is wise to fix a batten to the wall first upon which the base of the cupboard can rest (*Figure 28*). Then fix in the normal way. You now have an extra support which will take some of the strain off the normal fixing points. Never take chances! A heavy cupboard full of crockery can do a lot of damage if it leaves the wall.

If you have hollow walls, special cavity fixings (*Figure 29*) will have to be used – plus, preferably, the batten beneath each unit.

How to put up shelves

Three basic questions come to mind when shelving is discussed. Has it to be permanent? Does it need to look attractive? Do you want more than one?

If you live in a rented flat, or in temporary accommodation you may not wish to fix things to walls. In which case one of the designs in *Figure 30* may be useful. The first design makes use of an alcove, and it consists of bricks painted with emulsion on to which veneered chipboard shelves are rested. You can go to any height. An attractive alternative is to use glass jam jars and plate glass shelves. Be sure to get the edges smoothed before

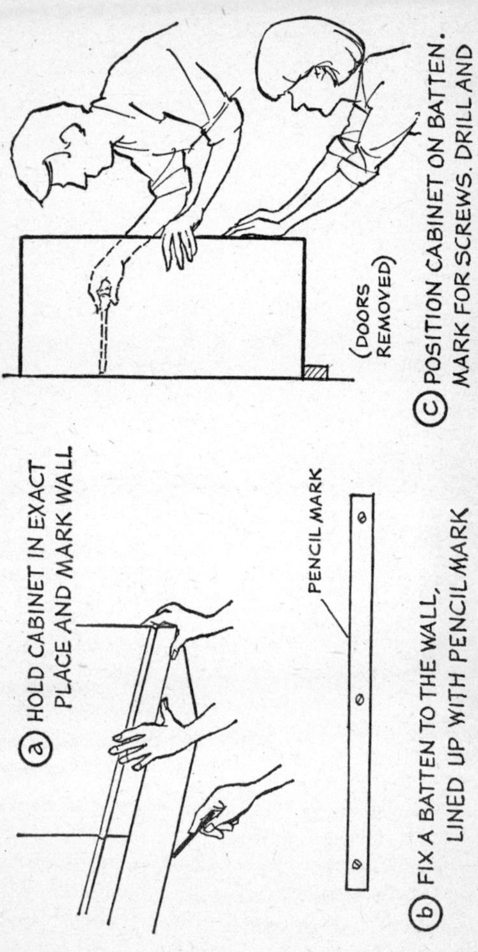

(a) HOLD CABINET IN EXACT PLACE AND MARK WALL.
(b) FIX A BATTEN TO THE WALL, LINED UP WITH PENCIL MARK
PENCIL MARK
(c) POSITION CABINET ON BATTEN. MARK FOR SCREWS. DRILL AND PLUG WALL. SECURE CABINET.
(DOORS REMOVED)
FIXING A HEAVY CABINET

Figure 28

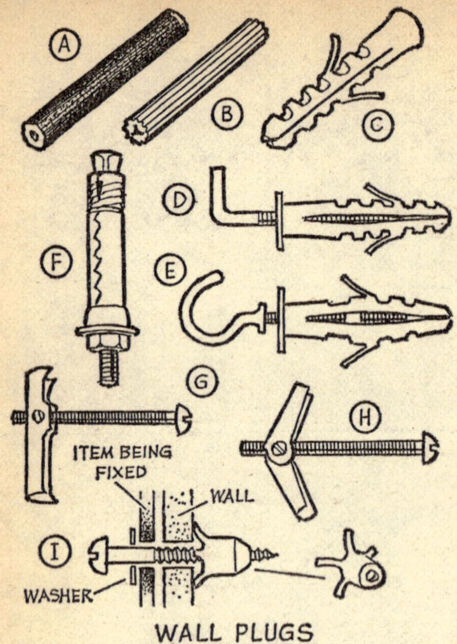

WALL PLUGS

Figure 29 **Key:** **A,** fibre wall plug. **B,** plastic wall plug. **C,** winged plug to resist turning. **D** and **E,** hook and plug combined. **F,** anchor bolt. **G** and **H,** cavity wall fittings. **I,** plastic cavity fitting.

using glass for shelving. Any good glazier will do this job for you.

The third design also makes use of the alcove, but in this case two side panels are of veneered chipboard. You will see they have ledges pinned and glued on them on to which the shelves will rest. No wall fixing is required, though it is wise if the shelves are tight enough to push the side panels against the alcove walls.

In the fourth design, the rope ladder technique is used to string shelves so they rest upon knots in the rope. The whole unit can then be suspended from the picture rail, or even hung on

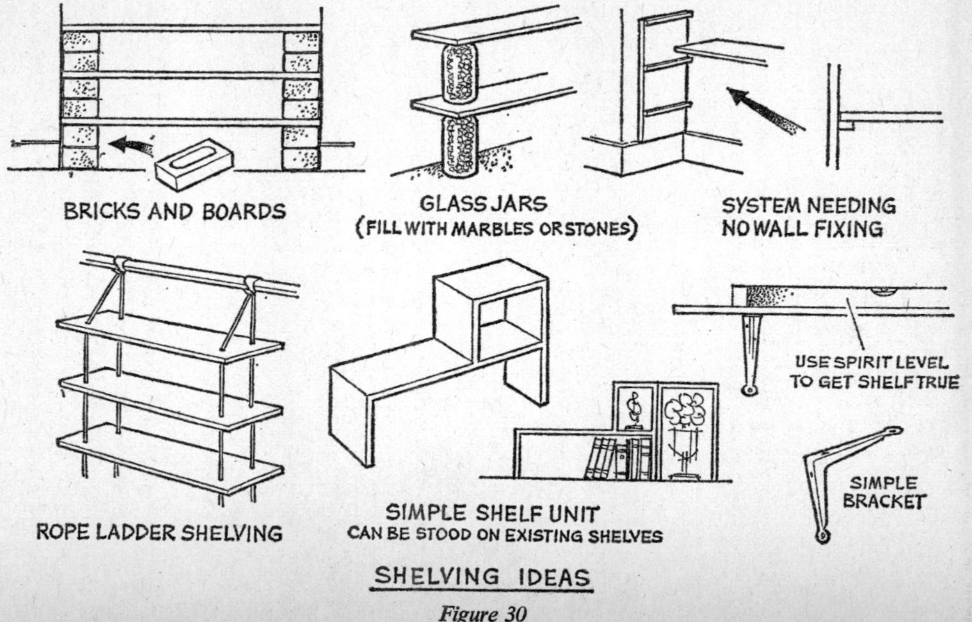

SHELVING IDEAS

Figure 30

the inside of a door, suspended from nails tapped into the top edge of the door.

Where making holes doesn't matter and appearance doesn't matter too much either, brackets such as shown in *Figure 30* will give a good strong fixing. The horizontal piece should be at least 25 mm (1 in) shorter than the shelf depth front to back. The vertical part is normally longer than the horizontal section.

Buy the screws when you get the brackets, and make sure they go through the holes easily. They must be long enough to go through the wall plaster and into the masonry behind, so they will need to be at least 37 mm ($1\frac{1}{2}$ in) long. Then you need as many wall plugs as you have screws to fit to the wall (not the shelf!). If the screws are number 8 size, ask for number 8 wall plugs. And then ask for a number 8 masonry drill. This is a special drill designed to cut into walls. It cannot be used on timber or metal.

You will also need something to put the drill in. Ideally, use a power drill which will make the work very easy. But if you can't get one, you need a wheel brace. Other tools needed are a screwdriver to fit your screws, a small hammer to tap the wall plugs home with and a spirit level.

Decide where the shelf is to go; how long it is to be, then mark roughly where the brackets will be positioned. Place them about 125 mm (5 in) in from each end. Hold just one bracket in position and mark through the holes on to the wall with a pencil point. Do be sure the bracket is vertical and that you have the longest section on the wall. Remove the bracket, now drill into the wall at least as deep as the length of a wall plug. Clean the dust from the hole, then tap in one of the plugs until it is flush with the wall. Now hold the bracket in place. Is the other pencil mark in the right place? You are checking just in case the drill tip wandered slightly and you need to reposition the other mark! Drill any other holes for this bracket, fit plugs, then screw the bracket to the wall.

Lay the shelf on the bracket; now get someone to hold the other bracket in place with the shelf resting on it while you check with your level to make sure the shelf will be level. Now mark for holes, drill and fix as before.

Rest the shelf in place, correctly spaced, then mark your

shelf on the underside to take fixing screws. Note these screws must be short enough not to come through the top of the shelf. It is wise to use a small twist drill just to make a start hole for the screws – but do be careful not to go right through!

Fixing laminate

Fixing decorative laminate is a very satisfying operation as long as you obey a few simple rules.

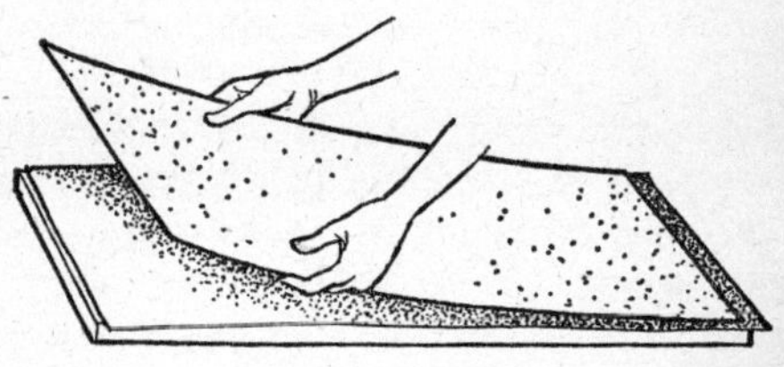

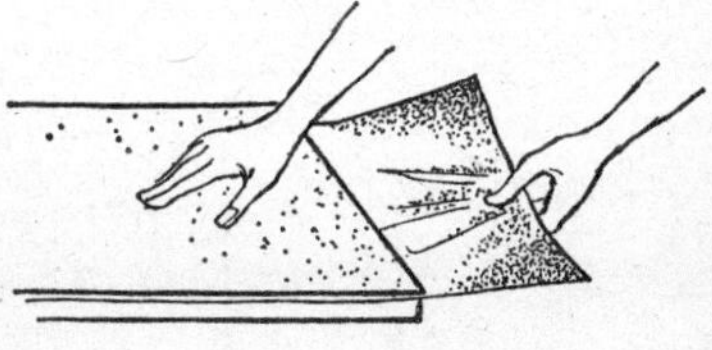

Figure 31

The simplest way to cut it to size is to use a straight edge and a craft knife fitted with a laminate cutting blade. Simply score the surface of the laminate until you are through the melamine surface, then snap the material upwards. It will break clean. You can shape corners with a fine saw, a sanding tool or a drum sander applied very gently.

Apply contact or impact adhesive to the underside of the laminate and the surface to which you are fixing it, and allow both to become touch-dry. Then lay a sheet of brown paper – or better still the release paper from self-adhesive plastic sheeting – on the unit and lay the laminate on top. It won't stick. When your laminate is accurately positioned, ease out the paper and you will have a perfect job (*Figure 31*).

Another way is to lay a batten of wood across the unit on to which you lay the laminate. Then ease out the wood. Yet another is to stick drawing pins in the end of the unit, sticking up so as to form a ledge against which you can position the laminate before lowering it. Experiment with a piece of 'dry' laminate and see which method you are most happy with – but do remember once those two treated surfaces touch they are very hard indeed to part!

With the laminate down, smooth all exposed edges with glasspaper wrapped around a block. You can of course edge with strips of laminate in the same way, making your top protrude the thickness of the laminate strip to give a neat finish.

Insulation

The basic purpose of home insulation is two-fold. First it prevents valuable warmth escaping from the house, and secondly prevents cold winds finding a way in. It has been likened to putting a tea cosy on a tea pot, but with fuel prices always climbing the potential savings are far greater.

Figure 32 shows the main areas where heat is lost in a home and gives a rough guide to percentages involved. The figures in brackets represent the percentage loss after insulation, so you will see there are considerable savings to be made.

Your main concern may well be which areas give the best saving on money spent, and this is a very wise approach, for the returns vary considerably. Let us work through the options open to us.

Draughts

Some fifteen to twenty per cent of the heat lost is caused by draughts, yet draughtproofing materials are among the cheapest

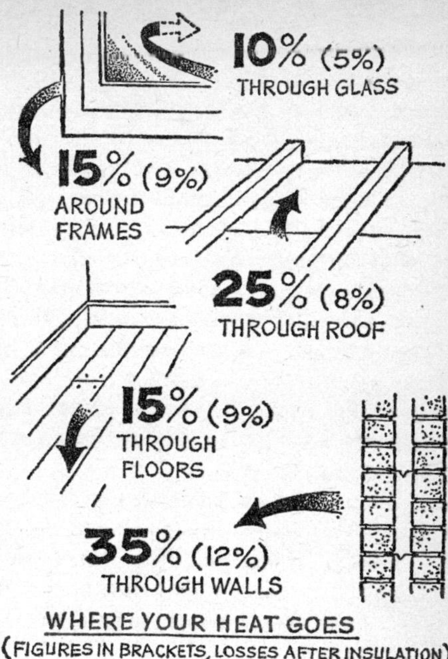

Figure 32

insulating materials. You can use a good quality foam strip with adhesive backing to seal gaps around casement windows. Or if you want something more durable, use sprung plastic or phosphor bronze strip pinned in place. This type of material can also be used on sash windows.

For the bases of doors, particularly exterior ones, you can buy special thresholds and baffles which cut draughts and also prevent rain blowing in. For interior doors you can get simple plastic flaps which are stuck in place, or a more sophisticated rise and fall draught excluder operated by the opening and shutting of the door.

A further fifteen per cent heat loss is through floors, and a proportion of that may be through gaps between boards or around the skirtings.

Seal small gaps with a proprietary filler, but for larger areas you can use *papier mâché*. This is shredded newspaper softened in water, then mixed to a pulp with glue size until a greyish putty is formed. Press this into gaps with an old kitchen knife with a flexible blade. Allow it to set then rub smooth with glasspaper. If you have to seal stained floorboards, then you can colour the *papier mâché* with a little water stain added to the mix. It will pay to experiment a little with colour, as stains often dry darker than you expect.

For really large gaps, a piece of batten, tapered a little, then coated with glue and tapped in the gap, will effectively seal them. When the glue has set, remove any surplus wood projecting with a small plane, a shaping tool or a drum sander.

It is worth mentioning here that double glazing is an effective form of draughtproofing – but it is by far the most expensive. But it has other benefits, see p. 84.

If your front door is exposed to winter gales, it is even worth treating the letterbox flap with a draught cover, and put a little flap over the keyhole. If you can afford it, the ideal draught-proofer is a porch built as an enclosed unit with another door. This will also provide somewhere to hang wet winter clothing and store boots etc.

Loft insulation

A lot of heat goes out through the roof, so it pays to invest in some form of loft insulation. And at the time of writing, in Britain, a Government grant of up to two-thirds the cost of insulation, not exceeding fifty pounds, is available towards the cost of the job. Regulations apply which deal with the need to insulate pipes and tanks, so check before you start the job. Local municipal offices can supply information and an application form if you are interested – but do bear in mind that you must apply for a grant before you do any work or buy materials. It will not be given for work already done.

You can choose between glass fibre blanket in rolls, either laid between joists or draped over them. Or you can use what is called a loose-fill, which is a granular material which can be vermiculite or expanded polystyrene, or a mineral wool, rather resembling dirty cotton wool. Aim to use 7·5 10 cm (3–4 in) of insulation – more if you can afford it. In Sweden 17·5 cm (7 in) of insulation is used in the loft space, but you could argue they have colder winters than us!

Stuff gaps at the eaves with mineral wool to stop draughts blowing in – and do remember to lag all plumbing against frost. It will be a lot colder in the loft once it is insulated. It also pays to leave a hole in your insulation immediately under water tanks so a little heat rises to keep the chill off them.

If you wanted to use the loft space, insulation can be applied to the rafters in the form of glass fibre held in place with insulation board if the roof is felted. That means you can see a layer of reinforced roofing felt hiding the roof tiles. If there are visible gaps between tiles, glass fibre is unwise as it would hold moisture. In this case, use an insulation board with a weatherproof face to the tiles. This is often a foil face.

But do remember that if you insulate the roof rather than the loft floor, you will now be paying to warm the whole loft area, which will add to your fuel bills.

Walls

There is not much you will be able to do here without calling in specialists, but the cavity in-filling of walls is a worthwhile, if expensive investment. About sixty to eighty per cent of your home is wall surface, and you can cut the heat lost by two-thirds with insulation. Choose a reputable company who will offer a choice of foam infill (which in very rare cases can lead to damp trouble), or a mineral wool infill which is applied dry, but which costs about twice as much as foam. The choice is yours, and I can recommend both systems. A good foam company will always advise you if they feel there are likely to be problems. Their reputation is as much at stake as your money!

If you have solid walls, you can have a lining of insulation board applied to the inside, but again I feel this is a job for the professional. There may be problems to overcome, such as the depth of skirting boards or door architraves, and the refixing of light switches and socket outlets. There isn't a lot you can have done from the outside, apart from the addition of vertical tiling, boarding or cedar shingles.

Double glazing

This is the insulation which needs careful thought, for with a ten per cent saving on investment it could take you thirty years or more to recoup your outlay! But double glazing has fringe benefits, for it drastically reduces the chilly down-draughts you often get by windows, giving you more comfortable living space. And it reduces or eliminates condensation on windows – one of the bugbears of our climate. It is also often stated that it reduces noise from outside, but do bear in mind that the spacing of glass for noise reduction is not the same as for heat insulation. The gaps must be considerably larger and the sheets of glass used of different thickness for sound insulation.

Of course, double glazing systems vary tremendously in cost. The simplest d-i-y systems using a plastic channeling around sheets of glass really cost little more than the cost of the glass. But a custom-made system fitted by a good specialist company will cost many hundreds of pounds. In between are many systems, and it will pay you to research the market carefully before making a final decision.

If you live in rented property where you don't wish to spend much, then draughtstrip, plus thick floorlength curtains will be almost as effective. In guest rooms you can fix polythene sheeting or clear plastic sheeting with double sided tape and it will do a good job even if it doesn't look as elegant.

With your home well insulated, it could tend to be on the stuffy side, so you must allow for ventilation. Extractor fans in kitchen and bathroom will remove steam and cooking smells, and you can plan to open windows during those periods when the heating system is resting. Don't allow your home to take on a stale fuggy smell, which you may not notice after a while – as your friends will!

A final word. It will pay you to insulate the hot water cylinder with a nice thick jacket, as heat loss here can be very expensive.

If you use the airing cupboard for clothes airing, arrange for one panel or flap to be openable. This will supply all the warmth you need without waste.

Damp

I think it is true to say that damp, in one form or another, causes more trouble in our homes than all the other problems put together. It damages the fabric, rots timber, ruins decoration and gives the whole place an unhealthy atmosphere.

There are three main areas of attack: up from the foundations; in through walls and roof, then an insidious hidden infiltration through moisture suspended in the air indoors. This latter causes what we call condensation, and it is often the most difficult to combat (*Figure 33*).

Let's look briefly at each.

The ground contains varying amounts of water according to the time of year. And, given the chance, it will rise into your house through floors and walls. To stop this, defences are built into the fabric of the house. Solid floors have a damp-proof barrier built into the concrete, and the walls have a horizontal barrier called a damp proof course (dpc). You can spot this in most houses just below the air bricks, but some really old properties may not have a dpc included.

If the barrier in the floor was poorly laid or is damaged in some way, you may find traces of damp coming through. This can usually be stopped by coating the floor with a special damp-resisting compound or paint, then for added protection you can lay a waterproof building paper over the paint while it is still tacky. You can get a paper with a foil-face, and this can be used with the foil side up so that it reflects warmth back into the room, helping insulation.

If the damp seems really serious, seek the advice of your borough surveyor, at your local town hall or municipal offices. Some form of drainage may be necessary to draw excess water away.

An added problem with floors is that you may have condensation trouble rather than rising damp. Here's a simple test. Clear an area of floor and make a hollow box (19–25 cm² [3–4 in²]) using putty as the walls. Lay a square of glass on the putty and press down to give a seal, with the glass about 2 cm (¾ in) from the floor. Leave in place overnight.

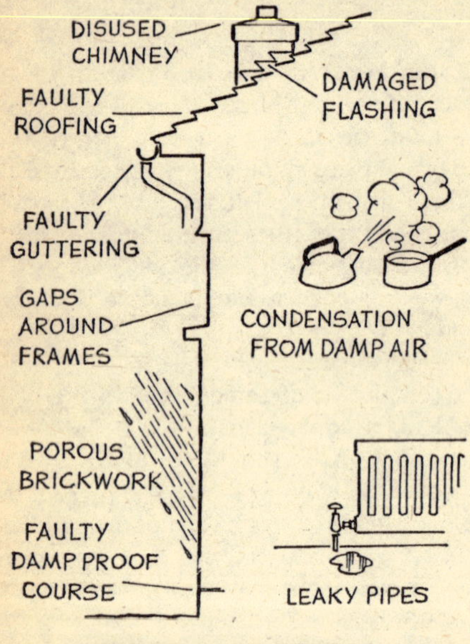

Figure 33

If you find moisture has condensed on the underside of the glass, there is rising damp. If moisture has formed on the top surface of the glass, it is condensation, which we will deal with later.

A suspected fault in the damp proof course is more of a problem. First ensure that nothing bridges the course – e.g. a flower border, heaps of sand or earth. This could be carrying damp above the barrier. And make sure paths are at least 15 cm (6 in) below the dpc, otherwise rain can splash up above the dpc also giving trouble.

How does one deal with a faulty dpc? There are special chemicals supplied as a liquid which can be absorbed into brickwork. Once in, they solidify, forming a barrier in depth which will keep damp at bay. Most of the systems are carried out by specialist companies, but at least one form can be hired at many hire shops, and includes a special injector to push the chemical under pressure into the wall. Obviously it is a lot cheaper to do it yourself, but if you decided to go to a specialist company, get two or three quotes from reputable firms, as prices do vary quite a lot.

Now what about the walls? Here, porous brickwork is often the culprit, and rain finds its way indoors. All bricks are porous to a certain extent, but they don't normally soak all the way through, and they dry out when the weather improves. You can treat porous walls, including the pointing, with a water repellent, which usually contains silicones. This is a superficial coating which stops damp going in while still allowing the wall to 'breathe'. Don't get it on window glass or paintwork, as it forms an invisible coating which is very hard to remove, and which eventually causes stains and smears. And also remember that these coatings cannot cure rising damp; in fact they can aggravate the problem.

You can also seal a wall by painting it with a good masonry paint if the wall is textured or rendered. Please don't paint attractive facing brickwork with paint, for once done you will never get it off if you later change your mind.

The problem of damp on walls may be aggravated by leaking gutters and down pipes, so check to see they are not faulty. The ideal time is during a really heavy downpour when you can see where rainwater is going. Often the problem is only a blocked pipe or gutter, often caused by birds nesting, but in older properties it may be rusted guttering or cracked pipes, or faulty gutter brackets. Whatever the fault, it must be put right, then the wall treated with a protective coating or paint.

The roof is a vulnerable surface, and because it is out of reach, it may never get any regular checking for loose slates or tiles. I don't recommend your climbing about on the roof, but you can get a fair idea of the state of the roof by using binoculars from up the garden or across the road. Look for slipped tiles or slates and cracks and gaps where there should be none. Look at the joint between the chimney stacks and the roof (the flashing – *Figure 33*) and note any cracks or missing pieces. Check for chimney stacks which look as if they are leaning, or pots which are damaged or leaning. If you are worried, call in a reputable builder to confirm your suspicions.

Never ignore roof trouble, for damp may be getting into the loft area without your knowing. Sometimes it makes its presence known by brownish stains on the bedroom ceilings. Watch for signs of damp during or just after heavy rain. It could be a false alarm because a loft area treated with wood preservative applied by an over-zealous operator can lead to stains on a ceiling. But the liquid dries out, giving no permanent trouble – apart from an annoying stain (*see* ceiling stains).

Now let's move inside. The faults we have been looking at can cause stains on wallcoverings, or the damp may push them off the wall, but once the cause of the trouble has been dealt with, the trouble shouldn't recur.

The more insidious problem is that of condensation. All air contains moisture droplets, and in small concentrations they are a positive benefit to health and to the well-being of your woodwork. But when you start to cook, run baths, do the washing up or wash clothes, you will see the steam produced seemingly disappearing into the air, where it is held in suspension. Warm air can hold a lot of moisture, but cool it by allowing it to contact a cold window, mirror in the bathroom or cold wall surface, and the air will have to drop the moisture as droplets of water. This is condensation.

Bear in mind that air moves around the house as hot air rises, so damp air may travel upstairs, carrying its invisible load of water. It may end up in the spare, unheated, bedroom, where it condenses on windows and walls. Leave the bathroom door open during or after a bath, and the same thing happens, so it is good practice to keep doors shut on kitchens and bathrooms while steam is being produced.

The logical step is to extract the moisture-laden air at source by means of an extractor fan, physically pushing the air out.

Opening a window may help, but if the wind force is on that window, air will merely come in, and your damp air will be pushed under the door into the rest of the house! I know you can argue that you are extracting warm air you've paid to heat, and this is true. Unfortunately, until we go in for air conditioning domestically there is little alternative.

Modern methods of insulation are deceptive, for while we may think we have cured a problem, it is quite likely to turn up somewhere else. For example, install double glazing – no more condensation on the glass – but it condenses on metal window frames and on cold wall surfaces. Fill walls with insulation and you get no further trouble on exterior walls, but the damp appears on the carpets of solid floors and on clothes in wardrobes, and, in severe cases, on bedclothes. Don't blame the insulation: you must remove the damp air.

There is a good chance that if you have full central heating and all your rooms are warm, you won't get much trouble as there are no cold surfaces. In fact, in a really dry home you may now need a humidifier to add moisture to the air!

And of course another cause of the problem is our success in draughtproofing our homes. In the old days with lots of air movement, and a big chimney flue over an open fire, we unknowingly pushed out the damp air in vast quantities. Now, with no draughts, few open flues and far more steam-producing appliances, no wonder we have problems!

Now to another problem. The air in your home is full of minute spores of various types of fungus, invisible to the naked eye, and quite harmless. But present them with a nice damp surface, such as the paintwork on your bathroom wall, or the grouting between the tiles – and they start to grow. They may not grow much, but they will form spots of colour we call *mould*. These stain the surfaces they grow on, and the marks may be impossible to remove. To kill off the mould you need to clean paintwork and treat bare walls with a proprietary fungicide used to correct dilution. Be sure to read the instructions and stick to the rules! Bleach may seem to have effect, but the trouble often reappears a few weeks later.

One form of mould it is hard to ignore is *dry rot*. This is a spore which likes dark, unventilated areas such as under the floor. If all the wall air bricks are kept clean so air can pass under the house, there is no risk, but if they become blocked, or you cover them over, the dry rot spore may grow into a large mushroom-like fruit, sending out tentacles to attack surrounding wood. It takes the moisture out of timber causing it to crack and

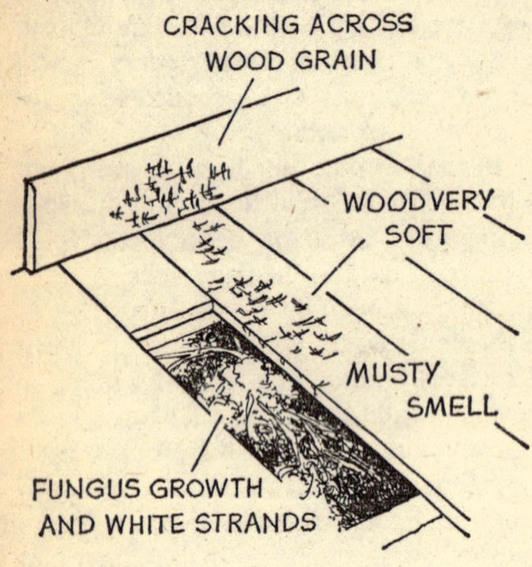

Figure 34

crumble (*Figure 34*), and you get a horrible dank, musty smell. Once it has got a grip, the attack spreads to dry, sound timber, and it has been known to spread from basement to roof in months under ideal conditions. If you suspect trouble, call in a specialist company which offers a free survey immediately. If you have trouble, they will quote for putting it right. This is not a job to do yourself.

Don't confuse dry rot with damp patches perhaps under a leaking radiator open to the room air. This may darken the wood and give signs of whitish strands growing, but it is only *wet rot*. If you cure the damp problem, the wood will dry out and the mould die off. If in doubt, ask the specialist company for a free survey. It will set your mind at rest.

Obviously, leaking pipes, tanks, radiators, toilets, can cause damp patches. Don't ignore any damp. Get it dealt with as soon as possible.

Should you meet a case of damp coming through a wall, or appearing on a chimney breast through damp coming from the inside of a flue, you can seal off the wall from the inside. There are special paints and papers which form a seal or barrier, over which you can decorate. But do remember that you have not cured the trouble. You may well be forcing the damp to move elsewhere where it can still get out. It still pays to deal with the damp at source.

In the case of a flue, it may be you have an unused chimney stack and the rain is coming down it. You need to get a half-round tile cemented over the pot to allow for ventilation but stop the entry of water – then add a small ventilator at the base of the chimney breast to allow for a small circulation of air. Normally, a flue will then dry out.

The house services

While it is not the purpose of this book to teach you all about electricity, gas and water in the home, I do want to say enough to take away any fear of their presence in the house. If you want to study electricity and plumbing, there are good books on the subject. Gas is the one service which is always left to the experts!

Let's look briefly at each in turn.

Electrics

Figures 35 and 36 show how electricity comes into the house, then how it is carried round. In an older house the system can be quite complicated, with a mass of fuses tucked away in boxes somewhere. In the modern home, the whole business has been simplified and all the fuses necessary will be housed in one neat box called a consumer unit.

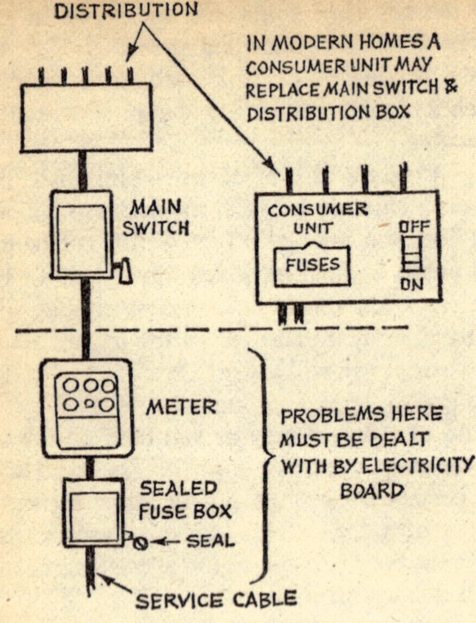

Figure 35

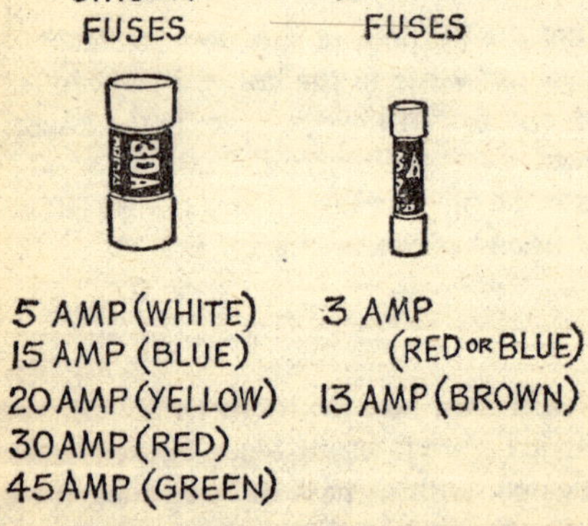

Figure 36

You will see that a cable has three wires (*Figure 37*). A red sheathed one, which indicates that it is the one carrying the electricity. A black one, which is the wire through which the electricity passes away from an appliance. And a bare wire or green or green/yellow sheathed wire which is called the earth wire. Should any fault develop, this is the wire which carries the

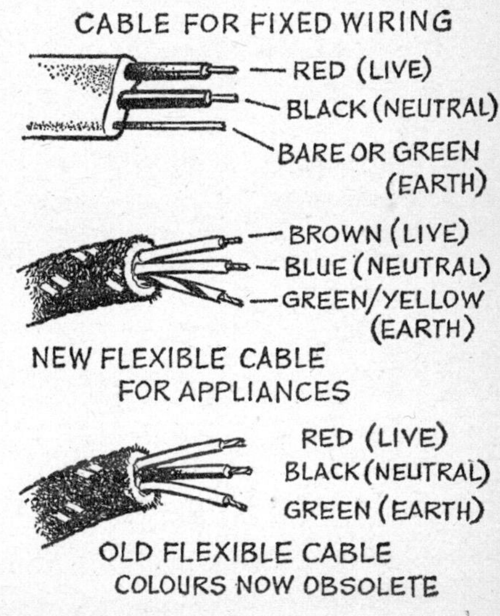

Figure 37

current to earth before it passes to earth through a human body.

The fuses act as a special weak link in any circuit so that if a circuit is damaged, by-passed or overloaded at any time, the fuse is destroyed and the current disconnected. In older homes there may be fuse carriers which are threaded with fuse wire of the correct thickness. You can buy the wire on a card, with the various ratings marked on the card. In more modern homes, the wire has been replaced by a cartridge in which a small piece of fuse wire is sealed.

Fuse ratings vary according to use, and the most likely for a consumer unit are shown in *Figure 38*. The only ones you will encounter when dealing with fused plugs are 3 amp and 13 amp, but if you have a consumer unit it is wise to keep spares for each in the box. It also helps to know which fuse is connected to which part of the house circuit. If in doubt, get a friend to help you mark them by pulling fuses and seeing what each controls

13 AMP PLUG
FUSE RATING CHART

3 AMP
SMALL DOMESTIC APPLIANCES :—
    HAIR DRIER
    IRON
    TABLE LAMP
    TV
    SEWING MACHINE
    TOASTER

13 AMP
LARGER APPLIANCES :—
    KETTLE
    FRIDGE - FREEZER
    LARGE FOOD MIXER
    ELECTRIC FIRES
    VACUUM CLEANER
    WASHING MACHINE
    POWER TOOLS

Figure 38

in the house. It makes it that much simpler to deal with a fault when one occurs.

Occasionally a fuse wire breaks down for no apparent reason, breaking a circuit. Merely replacing it with a new fuse of the same rating will cure the trouble. But if the replacement fuse goes also, suspect a fault in the system and don't use any more fuses until the fault has been put right by an experienced person. The only fault you can deal with is when too many appliances are connected to one circuit, overloading it and causing the fuse to melt. Merely disconnecting some of the appliances will be enough to put matters right, and a new fuse can be inserted. On no occasion must you put in a heavier fuse to stop the circuit breaking down. You are taking away the value of the fuse as a safety link.

You will find fuses in many plugs, and if an appliance fails,

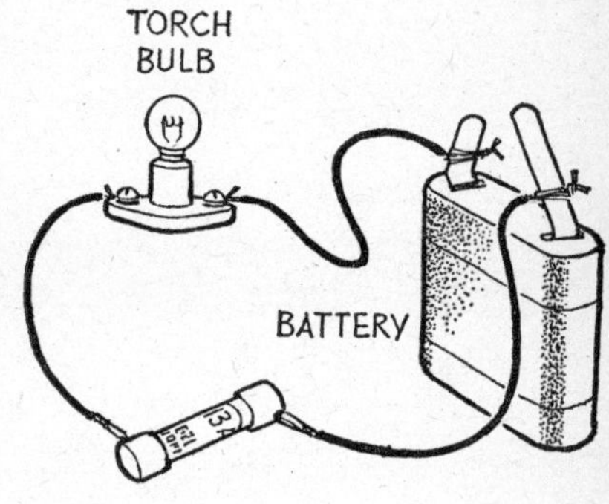

SIMPLE CIRCUIT FOR TESTING FUSES

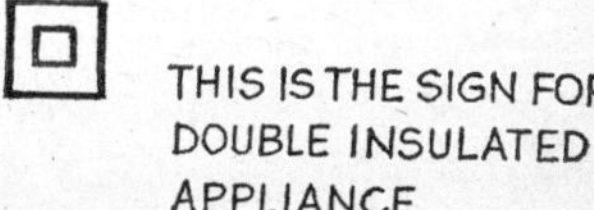

Figure 39

this is the first place to check. Take the cover off the plug by unscrewing the central screw, ease out the fuse and insert a new one of the same rating (check against the chart). Replace the cover and try the appliance. If it doesn't go, check both fuses with a simple circuit as shown in *Figure 39*. If they complete the circuit to the bulb, there is either a fault in the appliance or a fuse has 'gone' at the fuse box or consumer unit. If both fail to light the bulb, you have either used two dud fuses, or a fault has caused them to 'blow'.

Check a third fuse with your battery/bulb circuit. If it is

sound, insert it in the plug and plug in. If the appliance now works, you were harbouring some old dud fuses! Throw them away. If the fuse is blown yet again, there is definitely a fault in the appliance which must be repaired by an expert. You may argue this is rather an expensive run on fuses. Believe me, it is a

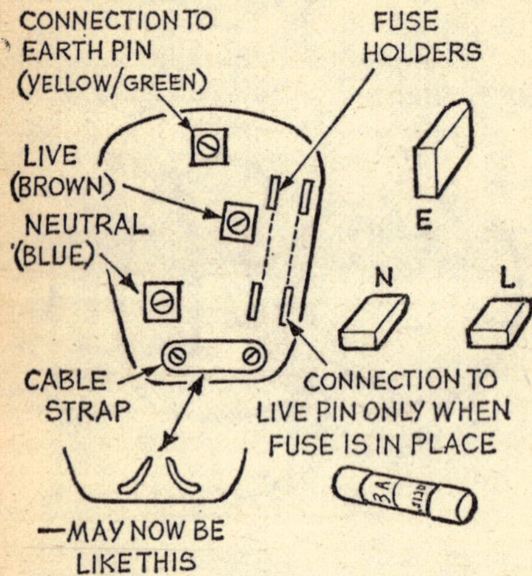

Figure 40

lot cheaper than calling in a service man or electrician when an appliance first ceases to work. You may well find yourself paying six to ten pounds only to be told that a fuse has gone in the plug! And that's a lot more than the cost of a couple of cartridge fuses.

You should also be able to wire a plug neatly and correctly. *Figure 40* shows the inside of a plug. The means of actually holding the wires may vary from plug to plug, but the position of the coloured wires is always the same. The colours are different from the cable colours already referred to in wiring circuits. Now we have brown for 'live', blue for neutral, and yellow/green for earth.

A cable stripper will help you get just enough sheath off each wire. Check to see whether the wires have to be the same length – or whether the earth one has to be longer to reach the top pin. If a screw device holds the wire, always wind the wire clockwise around the threaded pin. This will ensure that it isn't wound 'out' of the grip when it is tightened. And be sure to tuck in all 'whiskers' of wire. When you are sure all three wires are neatly housed, push home the cartridge fuse, anchor the flex in the holding device and replace the cover.

Some appliances are double insulated, which means that the electrical part is totally insulated from the outer casing and handle. With such appliances there is no earth wire, so you only have a live and neutral to connect. This is correct practice, but on no occasion should an appliance needing an earth connection be connected to a two-pin plug. You will always recognise a double insulated appliance by the little box within a box symbol somewhere on the casing (*Figure 39*).

While flexible cable gets its name because it can 'flex' or bend backwards and forwards, if it is bent too much the insulation may fail. This is the most common fault with an electric iron where there is a lot of movement near the handle. There should be a rubber grommet to reduce flexing, but if you smell burning, or see smoke come from the flex near the iron, or if there is smoke and the iron goes off – pull out the plug immediately. The flex has failed, and it may have blown the fuse in the plug as well.

It is not a very big job to take the back off the iron, disconnect the flex from the terminals, shorten the flex to cut out the damage, bare the wires exactly as they were before and reconnect to the correct points. But if you don't feel able to do this, get an expert friend to help. If the flex is too short to be cut back, take it to an electrical department and get a replacement flex of the same kind. Err on the long side if you have a choice.

With the new flex fitted, don't forget the fuse may have gone in the plug!

Often the amount of flexible cable supplied with an appliance limits the movement of that appliance. If you want to extend its range, buy an *extension cable*. This may be just a length of flexible cable in a plastic carrier, to which you must fit a socket one end and a fused plug the other. Or you may find one ready-wired to plug and socket. If you have the choice, buy a socket and plug of unbreakable rubber. They do cost a bit more, but it is money well spent.

Or you can buy an extension cable drum fitted with a plug, and with a socket built into the drum. This is the ideal way of extending a cable, especially out of doors. Be sure to read the instructions concerning using the drum with too much cable still wound on the drum. It can cause the cable to overheat.

When making up your own extension cables, remember the golden rule that a cable carrying current must always end as a socket. Electrical accidents always refer to a few people killed by touching a live plug on an incorrectly assembled extension cable.

Plumbing

Figures 41 and 42 show how water enters your house, and how it is likely to be distributed. In most built-up areas you will have a mixture of mains pressure – feeding the kitchen tap, perhaps bathroom cold taps and the storage tank in the loft – and tank pressure, feeding the hot taps and some cold taps. But in many country districts you may find that the whole system is mains fed.

There is a good reason for having storage tanks. It ensures an emergency supply should water be cut off, and it relieves the strain on a mains supply in a big city when everyone comes home from work and runs water. This could cause the mains supply to run dry!

The thing to remember is that the cold mains water is drinkable. The water from the storage tank is not. Even with a cover, it is not unknown for birds, mice and beetles to drown up there. So if you fill your kettle from a hot tap where the water is fed from a storage tank, it could be contaminated.

The different pressures do cause problems with ball valves,

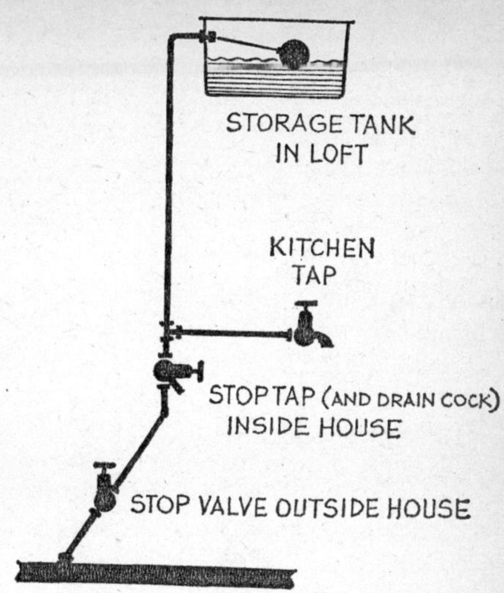

HOW WATER ARRIVES

Figure 41

shower units and water heaters where the cold and hot supplies are unbalanced pressure-wise. Be sure to raise this point when having appliances installed.

It is essential that you know where to turn off the water at the mains, and that the tap can be turned. It may be situated in a larder, under the sink – or wherever else the mains pipe rises into the house. And because it isn't used very often, it can become very hard to turn. Put some easing oil on the spindle of the tap, and work the tap until it turns easily.

You may find stop taps elsewhere, such as under the hot water storage cylinder. Ask someone experienced what they are for, what they control, and again be sure they will turn off. If you have an emergency with water, the first thing to do is to cut off the supply, thus limiting the amount of water you've got to cope with.

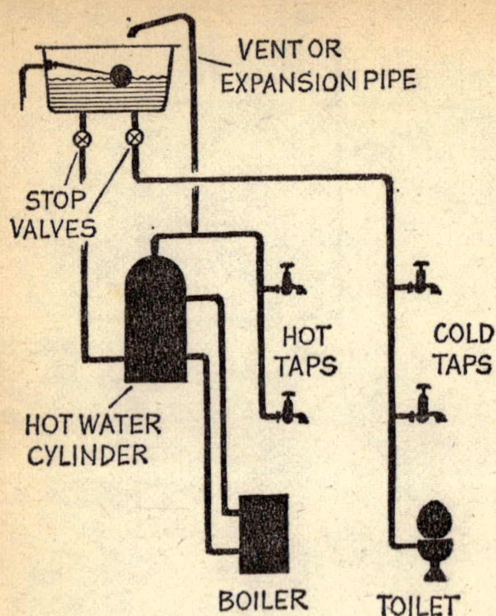

Figure 42

Taps *Figure 43* shows the three main types of tap, though styles may vary. The most important part is the washer, which when pressed down on to the seating cuts off the water. Modern taps give years of faithful service, but it is possible for washers to wear out. In older taps the seating may be a bit rough, and this can damage the washer.

Remember, for this kind of work you need a really big adjustable spanner with a long handle so you get plenty of leverage. And you need to be able to cut off the water supply to a tap before you can dismantle it. If you can't, get expert help. If the tap has a cover, you may need to remove the tap handle to get this cover off. The handle is usually secured by a small screw. Remove it, then use a rubber mallet to tap off the handle.

LOCKING NUT
CHECK VALVE
NOZZLE SEALING RING
VALVE SEATING
WASHER AND JUMPER
ANTI SPLASH DEVICE
SUPATAP
CAPSTAN HANDLE
GRUBSCREW
EASYCLEAN COVER
GLAND PACKING
JUMPER AND WASHER
NOZZLE
SQUARE SHANK
BACKNUT
PILLAR TAP
CRUTCH HANDLE
GLAND ADJUSTING NUT
GLAND PACKING
HEADGEAR
JUMPER WITH WASHER
VALVE SEATING
NOZZLE OUTLET
BIB TAP
TAP TYPES

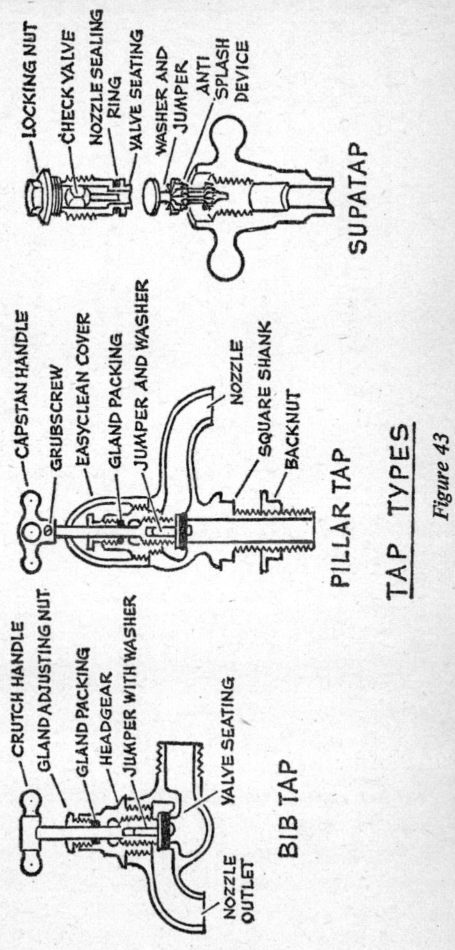

Figure 43

BALL VALVE TYPES

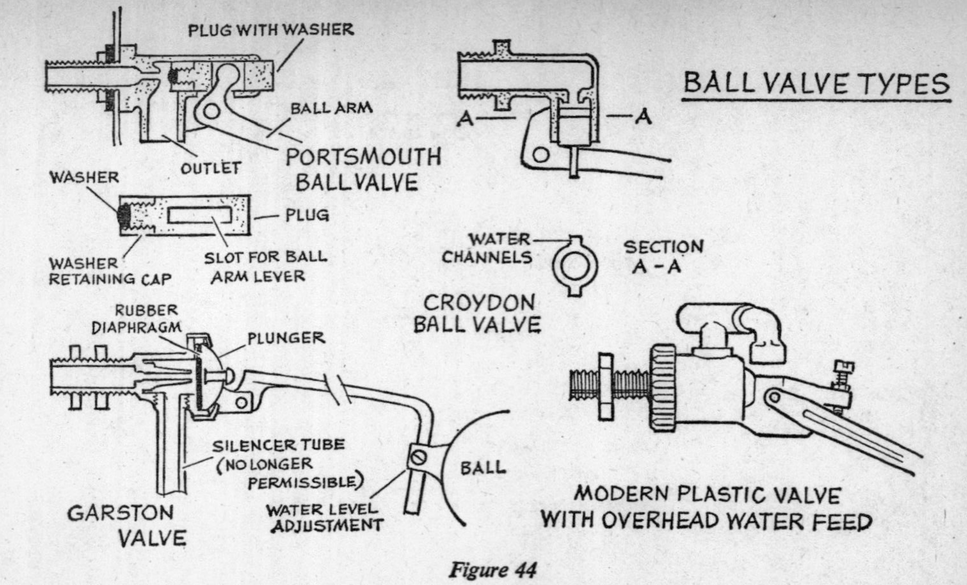

Figure 44

With the cover removed, unscrew the body of the tap. Be sure not to apply too much strain on a basin if the nut is tight. You may well crack it. With the tap apart, you will be able to see the washer and jumper. In a cold tap this jumper may be free just to pull out, but in hot taps the jumper may be 'captive' – that is held in the part of the tap that unscrews. If you have any problems, either with dismantling or with knowing what kind of washer to use, take the whole assembly to a plumbers' merchants or a good hardware department which has a plumbing section and seek advice.

Sometimes you may find water is merely weeping from around the tap spindle. This is caused by a fault in the gland packing, and often just tightening the gland packing nut will cure it. If this fails, remove the nut, add a little wool coated with Vaseline around the spindle, and replace the nut. Don't overtighten or you will find the tap hard to turn on and off.

Another kind of tap is the ball valve (*Figure 44*), which is used to

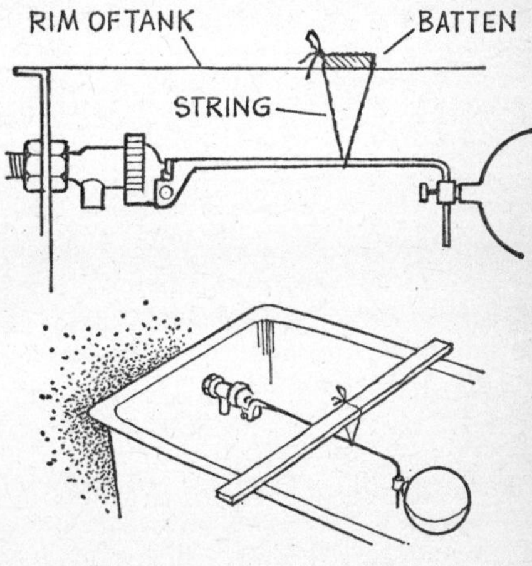

Figure 45

control water flow into tanks and toilet cisterns. Lift off a toilet cistern cover and you will find some kind of float attached to an arm, which in turn is linked to a valve. In modern systems this unit may be all plastic, and if you can turn off the water to this point you can unscrew the valve unit and have a look in. A piece of grit may be all that is stopping the valve working properly. Or the ball arm may have moved out of place and merely be catching on some obstruction.

In older properties, the ball may have corroded, in which case you can buy a modern plastic replacement. You can tie up the ball arm as shown in *Figure 45* if you don't want the water turned off until the valve has been repaired. Or the valve washer may need replacing – and here I would advise you to get in expert help to dismantle the valve unit. Usually a split pin will hold the arm in place, which in turn presses on the valve.

The ball valve used in a cold water storage tank will be of a similar type to that in the cistern. The only difference may be in the water control device, for as I mentioned earlier, mains pressure and tank pressure are not the same. Many modern replacement ball valve units have a choice of inlets – one for tank pressure, and a special restricting one for mains pressure.

Another area worth studying is the waste outlet to the sink or basins, for at some time one of these will get blocked. You will see there is a bend, called a trap (*Figure 46*), beneath the sink or basin, and this has a twofold purpose. First, it traps enough water to form a seal so that no smells can come into the house, or draughts blow up from an open waste pipe. And secondly, it forms a collecting point for debris.

In modern systems, the trap may be of plastic, and you can unscrew the trap. If the sink or basin is full of water, be sure you have receptacles to collect it before you remove the trap!

In older properties, the trap may be of metal, with a screw plug set into the end. This plug can be removed by using an old chisel blade to turn against the lugs.

With the trap open, remove all debris. A length of old curtain wire with a hook at the end is useful to clear anything left in the waste pipe. When clean, reassemble and flush through with hot water and detergent.

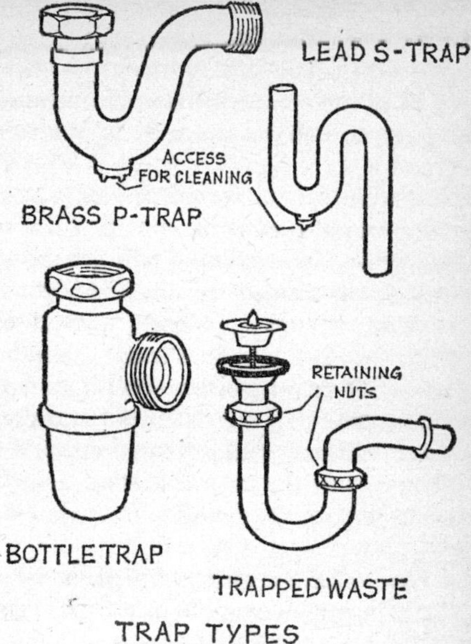

Figure 46

Central heating

You won't be expected to understand the complexities of the system, but there are aspects you should understand.

You will see a thermostat – or water temperature control – on most central heating boilers. This is set to control the temperature of the water you will use domestically, and 60 °C (140 °F) is about right. Any hotter and you merely have to add a lot of cold – and remember the hotter the stored water, the greater its heat loss. This control should be set and left alone. It is not an on-off switch.

There is another thermostat, probably in the hall, and this is set to the mean temperature required – say 20–21 °C (68–70 °F). If you listen, when it clicks off, it switches off the pump linked to the boiler. When it clicks on, it switches on the pump, which in turn activates the boiler flame. Having set this thermostat, it should not be touched. It is not to be used as an on-off switch for the central heating. The only time you can alter the setting is when you want to leave the central heating operating when you are out to keep the chill off the house. Then you can lower the setting.

It is also important to understand the time clock, for this is what turns the central heating on and off. There will be little tabs for switching on, and matching tabs for turning off, and the clock face will be marked for day and night. Remember the cost of running your system is going to be directly related to the setting of this clock, so think it out carefully. You may like it to come on half an hour before you get up or come home from work. But because the fabric of a house stores heat, you can turn off the system an hour before you go out or retire for the night. The period while the central heating is off is the best time for opening windows for removing stale air and freshening the place up.

While it is best to have a service agreement for the system to keep it in good condition, you can help by keeping the boiler free from dust.

Gas

As already mentioned, this is an area not to be touched. All you need know is where the on-off tap is for the gas supply and to ensure that you can operate it. You also need to know how to light and relight any pilot lights on your cooker and gas boiler or gas water heater, for these will go out when you cut off the gas. Remember never leave gas fires on when the gas is to be cut off.

If at any time you smell gas, check all appliances and open windows. If the smell persists, call the local gas board's emergency service and they will be around very smartly! Please don't search for leaks with a candle or matches, or while smoking.

Home security

About every three minutes, right around the clock, a house is broken into in Britain. But in a great proportion of cases it is more a case of walking in through doors left open, or climbing in through an open window. Even the most elementary precautions will discourage the amateur burglar, who knows there will be easier pickings elsewhere.

In the first instance it is a matter of playing safe. See you lock the doors, even if only popping to a local shop – or working down the far end of the garden. Close all downstairs windows at night. Don't leave keys in obvious places like under the mat; leave one with a neighbour if the children need to get in. Arrange for papers and post to be pushed in if you are away for a while, and stop deliveries. Don't leave notes for tradesmen to say you are away – and be sure to ask friendly neighbours to keep an eye out for you.

To improve your security, let's look at some of the defences you can add, starting at the front door (*Figure 47*).

A light over the porch, put on at night, will discourage anyone hanging around. Make sure the door is not hidden behind high hedges. Fit a peephole viewer in the door which will allow you to look out at a visitor without being seen. Only one small hole need be cut in the door to fit one.

Fit a good door chain held by long screws. This will allow the door to be opened just far enough to examine a caller, but the door has to be shut before the chain can be released. You can get locking chains so you can lock it on your way out. This adds a second defence to the door lock.

Most front doors are fitted with a simple rim lock and snick which, if the glass panel is broken, is merely turned by hand to open. Replace it with a deadlocking latch which, once the key has been turned and removed, cannot be released without the key. If you have doubts about the choice of a lock, there is probably a security or lock company in your area. Ask their advice. They may also recommend a good locksmith who will fit the new lock for you. It is not the easiest of d-i-y jobs. You will find there is

DOOR CHAIN
WINDOW LOCK
PEEPHOLE VIEWER
RACK BOLT
LIGHT IN THE PORCH
DEADLOCKING LATCH
SECURITY IDEAS

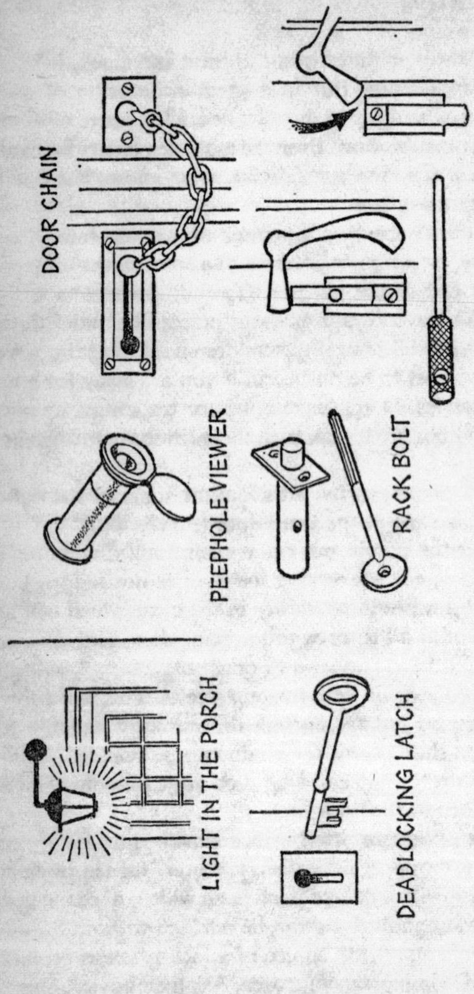

Figure 47

a police officer specialising in home security at your local police station. Seek his advice too if you have any security problems. He will be delighted to help.

In addition to the new lock, you may feel a couple of stout bolts will add extra protection. These can be the normal pattern of bolt, or you could fit what are called rack bolts. These fit into the edge of the door, and on the inside face of the door all that is visible is a small hole into which a special rack key is fitted to turn the bolt. The same type of bolt can be used on your back door.

The back door will also benefit from a better quality dead-locking latch so that the bolt cannot be released by breaking glass and putting a hand in. And please remember to remove the key at night or when you leave the house!

Glass is always a problem for it is a weak spot in the defences, so you may care to get the pane replaced in favour of a piece of laminated glass. It costs nearly three times the price of ordinary glass, but you really do need a pickaxe to make even a small hole in it. Alternatively, you can buy a special transparent film which is stuck to the glass to give it added strength. You can of course crack the glass, but you can't force a way through it.

If you want real protection, ask about hinge bolts. These are special bolts which go in the hinge side of a door to prevent a determined burglar using a jemmy on the hinges and levering the door open.

Windows are a common form of entry. Break a small pane, insert a hand and open the window. You can make the job far more difficult by fitting even a simple lock to the window. The most common for a casement window merely prevents the cockspur handle moving, while another type fits on the casement stay and locks it in place. For sash windows, you can either lock the window in the shut position, or fit a device which allows a few inches for ventilation – but no room for someone to climb in. There are types for metal and timber frames, and if you want locks, find a store which stocks a range and find something which meets your needs.

Then there are special locks for sliding patio doors, garage and shed doors and back gates. Ask to see these if you have a particular problem.

Just a word of warning here. It is not wise to lock internal doors and wardrobes and drawers when you go away. Should someone break in, they will not be deterred by locks if they have time to work, and you can end up with a tremendous amount of damage to furniture. Far better leave everything inside unlocked, but remove all valuables into safe keeping.

For small items like jewellery and valuable documents, you can buy domestic safes either to fit in the floor or into a brick wall. These may have a key or a combination which you can set yourself.

I am often asked about burglar alarms. Well, there are some excellent domestic systems on the market, but all suffer from the same snag. They must be well maintained and the battery renewed when necessary. And an alarm must be kept primed. This may be quite simple with a couple out at work all day, but it is well-nigh impossible in a family with children coming and going at all hours. In a recent report, the police stated that well over ninety per cent of all calls prompted by a domestic alarm were false alarms, and they were getting fed up!

So, if you fit an alarm, use it correctly, service it well, and notify your neighbours what it means! In their favour, it has been proved that one alarm triggered off in a road will ensure the safety of the rest of the road – for that occasion at least. Again, if you want advice, ask your local security officer.

Apart from protecting doors and windows, there are simple magnetic switch devices which will trigger off a siren if disturbed. These are useful for protecting a car, or in fact any object likely to be taken away without your consent. You will find these alarms in many security shops, but remember the weak spot is the battery. See that it is renewed at regular intervals so that the alarm really will go off when needed.

4

Domestic emergencies

No emergency situation around the house is half so bad if it has been anticipated. It is that feeling of panic and helplessness which is to be dreaded. So the first essential is to consider the kind of things likely to lead to an emergency situation, then have some accessories around which would be useful in the event (*Figure 48*).

Have a good torch with fresh batteries located where you can find it in the dark. Have an emergency light source – bottled gas lantern, or at least night lights and matches, located in a place where you can find them – and not to be taken away! See that you have a selection of spare light bulbs of various required wattages. As one is used, get another spare. Check that you have a selection of cartridge fuses, or, in an older house, a card of fuse wire. If you have spare fuse wire carriers, wire them up ready and mark what they're wired with.

Invest in a good dry powder fire extinguisher which conforms to British Standards (BS) and fix it near the kitchen. And a small domestic fire blanket in a holder is also a wise investment.

Have the numbers of the emergency services handy somewhere – gas board, central heating service department, a good local plumber. Fire brigade, ambulance service and police are of course available through the 999 service.

Now for a few tips:

TELEPHONE NUMBERS
PLUMBER
FIRE
DOCTOR
POLICE
FIRE EXTINGUISHER
60W
60 W
100 W
FIRE BLANKET
GAS
FUSEWIRE
FIRST AID
KEPT FOR EMERGENCIES

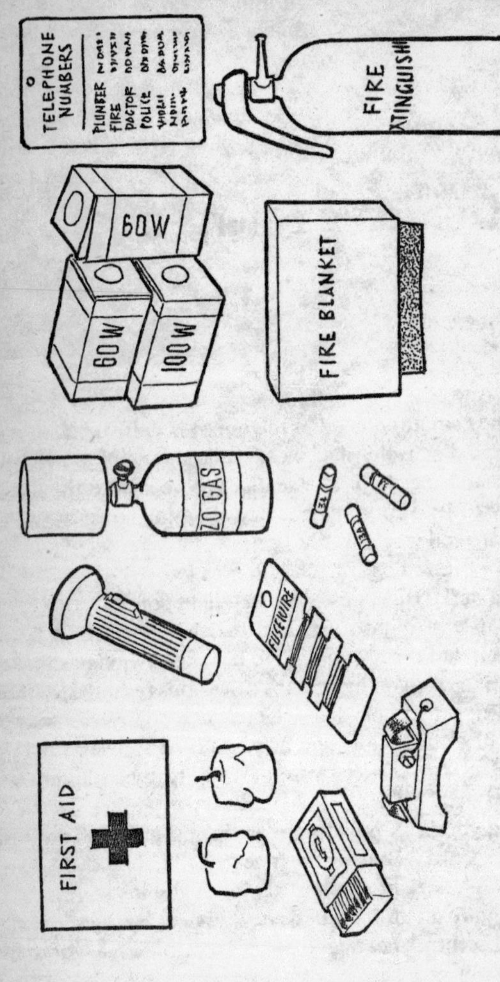

Figure 48

Lights go out

Check outside to see if neighbours' lights are out. It could be an area power cut.

If they are all on, check other rooms. It may be just a lamp which needs replacing. If other lights don't work, suspect a fuse. Check the fuse which controls the lighting circuit. If it is a lighting circuit fuse, you can plug in table lamps and standard lamps and use a power circuit.

If changing fuses doesn't help, and if all power circuits are dead too, it looks like a fault in the supply to the house. Phone your local electricity board and explain the problem. On no account break the seal on the company fuse.

If it was a general power cut, remember all electric clocks and time clocks will be slow.

If a table lamp or standard lamp goes out, try a new bulb. If this doesn't work, check the bulb in another holder. If it works, the lamp is at fault. If it has a fused plug, change the fuse (3 amp). If this fails, check the wiring on the lamp with the lamp *unplugged*. Sometimes the flex gets trodden on and pulled from the lamp or the plug.

Gas leak

If you smell gas, open windows, turn off all appliances and ring the emergency gas service. If you just suspect a leak, turn off all appliances and all pilot lights to cooker, boiler and water heaters until you are sure no gas is on. Now look at the dial on the gas meter. If it is moving there is a gas leak between the meter and the appliances. Call the emergency service of the gas board in your area immediately.

Water leaks

If you find water coming through a bedroom ceiling, turn off the water at the mains at once, then run all taps and flush toilets to reduce the water level in the tank in the loft. The tank may have rusted, and you will need a plumber to fit a new tank. If the ball valve fails, you may find water pouring from an outside overflow and you will hear water feeding to the tank. The overflow is put in a prominent place for this very reason – so you won't miss it when something goes wrong.

Again, turn off the mains tap, and run all taps and flush the toilets to reduce the water level in the tank. If you can get in the loft, once the water level is down in the tank turn on the mains then hold the ball valve arm up. If the water still flows you have a faulty valve. If the water cuts off, the valve may just be dirty and jamming, or it may need slight adjustment so the water doesn't get so high in the tank.

Dripping taps

Not so much of an emergency. See chapter 3 on services (p. 100).

Chip pan fire

Keep calm. Leave the pan where it is and cover it with a damp tea towel or even a large pan lid to snuff out the fire (*Figure 49*). Be sure to turn off the gas or electricity under the pan. If you have a fire blanket, drape this over the pan, holding it so you don't expose your hands to the flames. Never, never try to carry the pan out of doors. The flames may blow back at you or you may have to drop the pan because it is too hot. Never carry it to a sink – especially a plastic one. Never use water on oil. Should it get out of hand through spillage, leave the kitchen at once and shut the door behind you. Ring for the fire brigade at once.

If the fire is quite small and you have a fire extinguisher, use this to smother the fire. Try to save some of the contents in case the fire re-ignites because of the heat from the metal pan.

House fire

If you find a fire which cannot be dealt with by a domestic extinguisher, or if you have no extinguisher, get all occupants out as quickly as possible, shut all doors and call the fire brigade. If the fire prevents your getting downstairs, get the family into a

Figure 49

bedroom, shut the door and block it at the bottom to keep out smoke. Open a window and shout for help.

As a precaution at night, check that all cigarette butts are out, that any open fire has an adequate guard and that radios and television sets are unplugged – not just switched off.

Locked out

It always pays to have spare keys with a friend, or hidden away somewhere well away from the house where they would never be found by a casual searcher. This is even more important today when we are more security conscious. Failing all else, look up a locksmith in Yellow Pages. They too run emergency services.

You may be able to get in by breaking a small pane of glass near a window catch, or by getting a small boy to climb in through a small window left open. But bear in mind for the future you have two weak spots in your defences. If you can do it, so could a crook!

Unwelcome callers

This is a very tricky problem, for many thieves now gain entry by posing as official workmen come to check your house.

If you are on your own, use a door chain. If you are not expecting a caller ask to see his identity card. You have no way of knowing if it is forged or stolen, so ask the person to wait while you look up their department in the phone book and ring to ask if their men are in your area. If they know of no work in your area ring the police. He may already have gone when you say you are checking. In which case ring the police and explain.

If you are minding keys for a neighbour on holiday, never let workmen have these keys, or let them in the house unless you have had clear instructions from your neighbours. Don't be fooled by 'nice men'. It is their business to look neat and be polite – and they make enough money to be able to afford to dress well!

Don't be fooled by men in uniform – even policemen – asking to come in. Don't be afraid to ring and check them out. Your action could save scores of gullible people.

If you feel unsure what to do, ring a neighbour and involve other people in the situation. No criminal will welcome witnesses who could identify him.

Blocked drains

This can be an unpleasant business, but one which plumbers are well used to dealing with. Stop feeding water into the drains and flush toilets as little as possible and call for help from a plumber. There are specialist drain clearing companies, but get some idea of costs before calling one out. Because they run a twenty-four hour service, their overheads can be very high – and this will be reflected in their charges.

Broken window   (*Figure 50*)

If a pane is just cracked, use waterproof glazing tape to seal the crack. This will see you over until the pane can be replaced. To my knowledge there is no adhesive which will successfully repair a broken pane of glass.

If it is badly smashed, wiggle out all the broken pieces. Wear a heavy leather gardening glove, and use pliers for obstinate bits and to remove any small glazing sprigs. Clean out the rebate and fit a piece of hardboard in the frame until you get your glass. If the hole is near a window catch, play safe by wiring up the handle or catch so the window can't be opened.

When you measure for the new glass, take 3 mm ($\frac{1}{8}$ in) from each dimension so the glass is not a tight fit in the hole. This is so it can be cushioned by putty against knocks. If you have doubts about the weight of glass you need, take a scrap piece with you to the glazier. He will know what to supply.

You also need fresh putty, and again he will advise how much is needed. If you are dealing with a metal frame, remember you need metal casement putty as ordinary putty won't dry out on metal frames.

Apply priming paint to a wood frame prior to glazing, then put in a bed of new putty on to which the glass is pressed. Always press around the edges of the glass – never in the middle. Then use a few glazing sprigs to secure the glass. Tap them in place with a small hammer, sliding it against the glass so you don't damage it. Make sure they won't be visible above the wood frame. Finally you need a bead of finishing putty – and this is the tricky part as there is an art in getting a neat slope. You can buy a little glazing tool which will help you with this job if you can't manage with a standard putty knife.

Metal frames need the same basic treatment except that the glass is often secured with special little glazing clips. You will encounter these when removing the broken glass – if there are any to refit.

Leave the putty for two weeks before painting.

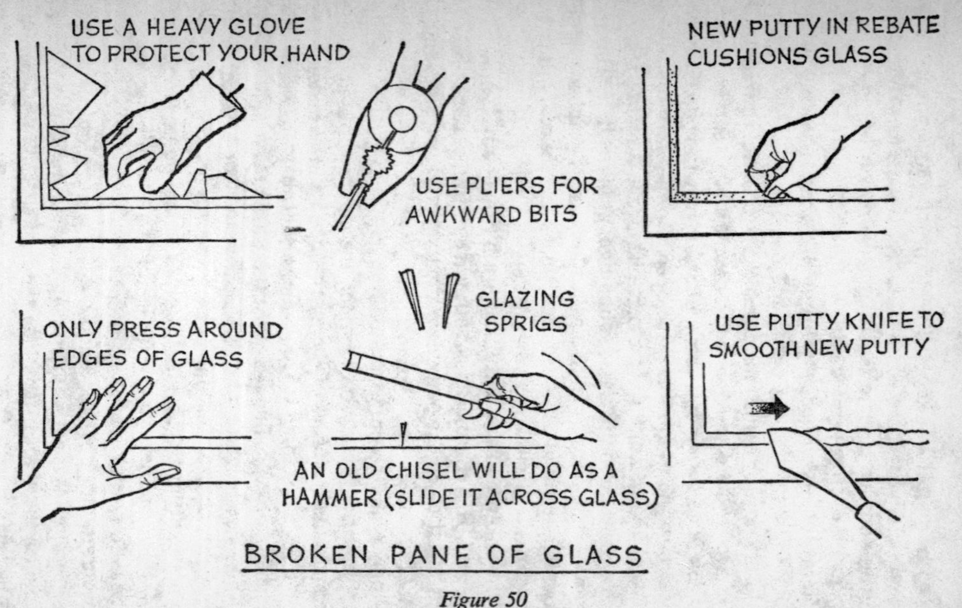
USE A HEAVY GLOVE TO PROTECT YOUR HAND
USE PLIERS FOR AWKWARD BITS
NEW PUTTY IN REBATE CUSHIONS GLASS
ONLY PRESS AROUND EDGES OF GLASS
GLAZING SPRIGS
AN OLD CHISEL WILL DO AS A HAMMER (SLIDE IT ACROSS GLASS)
USE PUTTY KNIFE TO SMOOTH NEW PUTTY
BROKEN PANE OF GLASS

Figure 50

Spilled paint

If you spill gloss paint on a carpet, keep it damp with turps substitute or white spirit. Failing that use a proprietary paintbrush cleaner. The paint mustn't be allowed to set in the fibres. Use plenty of clean rag and paint remover to get the paint out. Finish off with warm soapy water to remove the chemicals from the fibres. Carpet shampoo will do too.

If you spill emulsion paint, again keep it wet. Don't let it set. Use lots of water to dilute and remove it.

Once paint has set, it is hard to soften. A paintbrush restorer will help, but it pays to test it out first to make sure that it won't affect the colour of the carpet.

Remember when decorating out of doors that the best time to clean up splashes of paint from tiles and paths is while it is wet. Once set, it is hard to move.

Grease on wallpaper

Anything spilled on vinyl wallcovering or a wipeable paper is easily removed, but splashes on normal paper are a different matter. Place blotting paper over the grease marks and apply a warm iron so the blotting paper takes up some of the grease. A 'rubber' made from bread dough is also a help, but whatever remains after these treatments is not going to come off. It will have soaked right through. You may have to disguise it by putting a patch over the top. Make a patch by tearing wallpaper so that the tear is under-cut and thus very thin at the edges. Paste it down and the edges will merge well into the surrounding paper. Cut edges never will.

Freeze-ups

Unless your plumbing is well lagged, and especially if you have now insulated the loft so the space up there is colder – you could get frozen pipes during a really severe spell of cold weather. Often, no damage is done, apart from a slight distortion of a lead pipe, or a stressed joint on a copper system.

If you can locate the frozen area, apply hot rags to it or the warmth of a hair dryer. Never use a blowlamp or an open flame because of the danger of fire.

If you can see ice glinting through a damaged pipe, buy a glass fibre repair kit and do a repair using filler and glass bandage before the pipe thaws out. Look upon this as a temporary repair until a plumber can do the job properly.

Where damage is not discovered until the pipe thaws, and you have a real leak, turn the water off at the mains if it is a mains-fed pipe, or drain down the storage tank if it is a tank-fed pipe. Then call in the plumber.

Looking to the future, lag all exposed pipes.

5

Useful hints and tips

Very often it is the little wrinkles rather than the big articles which make work that much easier or save money. Here are fifty I have found useful over the years.

1. To stop paint skinning in the can, lay a circle of foil on the paint surface before closing the can. This will exclude air which causes skinning. Or transfer small remains from a large can into a jar which just holds it so that no air is stored. Don't turn the can upside down. This merely means you get skin on the bottom instead of the top!
2. Always mix paint well before use. If it is bitty, transfer the paint to a clean can or jar, then fix a piece of clean nylon stocking over the mouth of the jar and push down into the paint. The paint will automatically be strained as it is used.
3. A paint 'kettle' with handle is useful for holding paint. If you have to change colour, line the kettle with aluminium foil before using. Then when you need to change, pull out the foil liner and you have a clean container (*Figure 51*).

4. Don't leave paintbrushes for any time in water. It gets into the stock of the brush and it can rust the metal ferrule. If you must leave them, load them with paint then wrap in kitchen foil to exclude all air (*Figure 51*).

5. When brushes have been cleaned, slip a loose elastic

Figure 51

band over the bristle tips to help keep a good shape. Store in a warm, dust-free place to dry.

6. If you have to cut wallpaper to a shape, cut it dry. Wet paper tears very easily. The exception is when using vinyl wallcovering which is tough enough to be cut after pasting. Trimming at rail and skirting will have to be done wet, so be sure to have sharp decorating scissors.

7. Where an irregular surface is encountered you may have to cut to lose creases. Always tear the paper rather than use scissors, as the irregular edge is far

more likely to blend in with the pattern. The same applies when patching. Tear the paper so that it has a feather-edge which doesn't throw shadows.

8.   Vinyl wallcovering may not go down at the seams if there is a slight overlap as the paste doesn't bond to the vinyl. In such circumstances, wait until the edge is dry then use a clear resin adhesive along the edge. Don't spill it on the vinyl as it may attack it.

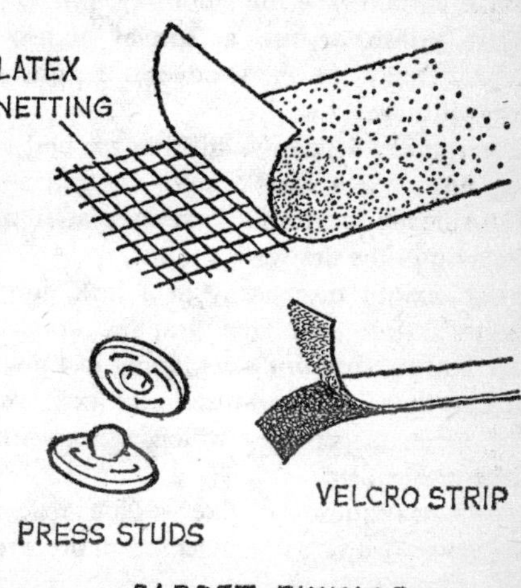

Figure 52

9.   To stop a rug or mat sliding on a polished floor, use Velcro strip stuck to floor and rug. This double tape grips itself firmly by means of thousands of little hooks and loops – but it can be ripped apart without damage to rug or floor.

10. Stop carpets 'creeping' by using a special latex netting or a bristle-faced strip (*Figure 52*). The netting offers yet another way of stopping mats sliding on polished floors. Stair pads on open tread staircases can be held in place by special press studs; one half is screwed

into the tread and the other is sewn to the underside of the carpet.

11. Be sure to remove all old tacks and pins from a timber floor before laying new floorcoverings. A simple final check can be made by slipping a nylon stocking over your hand and running it lightly over the floor surface. The stocking will very quickly snag on any projection.

12. To make curtain rails run smoothly, rub with silicone furniture polish or use a special aerosol silicone lubricant. Don't use oil. It collects the dust and goes gummy with age.

13. Drawer runners which are sticking are best lubricated by rubbing with a candle stub. Or you can use an aerosol silicone lubricant. Take care after treatment! You may pull the drawer right out.

14. If a key doesn't turn easily in a lock, lubricate the mechanism with powdered graphite applied with a puffer. To lubricate tumblers, apply just a spot of oil to the key, then insert and turn in the lock. Don't apply lots of oil. It attracts dust which, mixed with oil, will clog the mechanism.

15. For delicate equipment like sewing machines and clocks, only use a very fine machine oil prepared for the job. Normal oil can clog up the mechanism. Apply on a pin or shaped matchstick. Only the smallest amounts are needed.

16. If a screw is very tight and doesn't want to move, try tightening it a fraction more before loosening. If the head is clogged or sealed with paint, clear it with a knife blade before trying to undo the screw.

17. Where rust has a grip on latches or catches, don't try force. Apply a little easing oil to the working parts and wait for it to loosen the joint. Clean off once free and apply lubricating oil.

18. Large nails which seem impossible to pull out may best be dealt with by hammering them down through the wood until the wood can be released. Then you can

pull the nail with the claw of a hammer. A nail punch is useful for this job.

19. Rusted bolts will often succumb to treatment with easing oil. Where a nut is impossible to remove, there is a tool you may be able to borrow called a nut splitter.

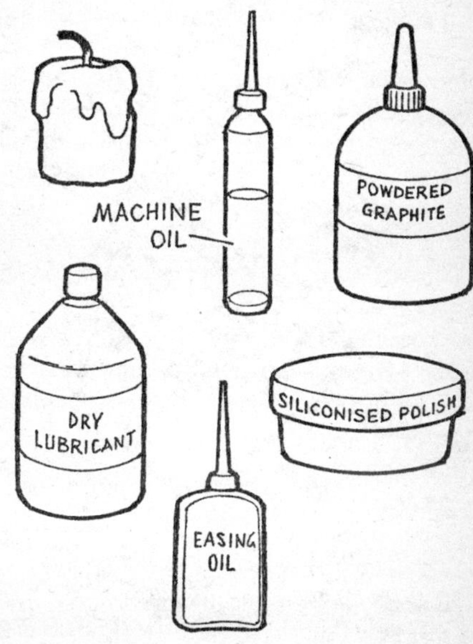

USEFUL LUBRICANTS

Figure 53

This can be used to cut the nut without damaging the bolt thread. You will of course need a new nut.

20. If you have to drill a ceramic tile, stick a small piece of adhesive tape over the spot to be drilled. This will hold the masonry or glass drill in place while a hole is started. Drill as slowly as you can at first.

21. Remove scuff marks on vinyl tiles with fine wire wool lubricated with turps substitute. Then polish in the

normal way to remove any dullness you may have created.

22.   Make simple throw-away brushes for adhesives by threading coarse string through an old piece of copper tube. Or for finer brushes use an old ball point pen case with the refill removed. The soiled string can be pulled through and cut off (*Figure 54*).

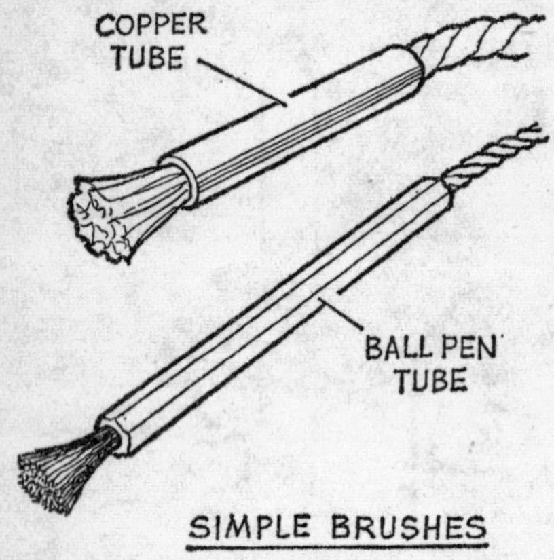

Figure 54

23.   To hold small tacks in place while you tap them with your hammer, push the tack through a piece of scrap card. Then tear the card away once the tack is firm. A piece of Plasticine or similar material can be used if you want both hands free (*Figure 55*).

24.   A simple way of dividing a width into a required number of equal parts where the full width is not equally divisible, move your rule diagonally until you can read off a measurement easily divisible by the number required. *Figure 56* shows you how.

25.   If you have to join polythene sheet, don't use adhesive as none will stick it. Use a warm electric iron over a piece of aluminium kitchen foil and weld the material. If you have a lot to do you can buy a little electric

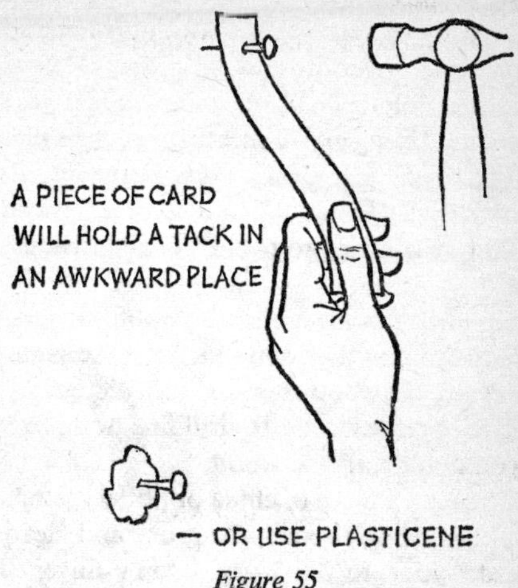

Figure 55

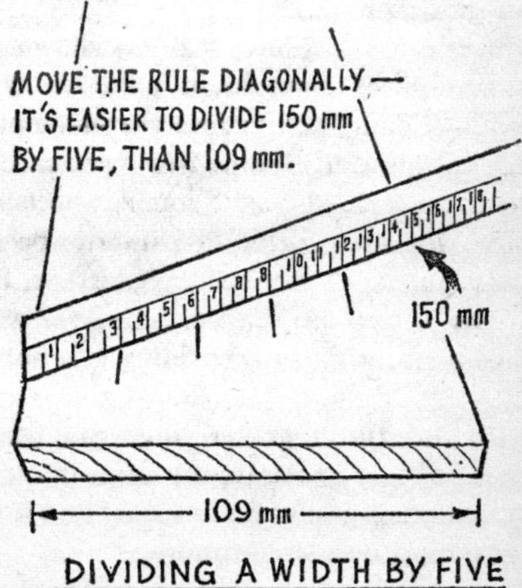

Figure 56

tool to do the job. It resembles a soldering iron with a wheel at the tip.

26.   If you want to make covers with polythene sheet, invest in a simple eyelet kit and clip these to the sheet at set intervals. Polythene on its own will tear easily.

27.   To repair damaged pvc sheeting – such as plastic macs – use a special pvc repair tape. Although it resembles self-adhesive plastic tape, it has a special adhesive which bonds firmly to pvc. PVC adhesive is also available.

28.   When nailing along a piece of wood, be sure to stagger the nails so that they don't all enter the same grain run. If they do, the wood may well split along this grain line. In hardwood it is wise to drill fine holes for your nails so you don't split the wood.

29.   If you break a piece of china or pottery, store the pieces in a plastic bag to keep them dry and clean until you can do your repair work. Don't finger the pieces. Assemble the item dry and number or letter pieces before starting to glue.

30.   As a temporary measure, seal cracked panes of glass with waterproof transparent adhesive tape. It will prevent any damp getting into the frame until you can replace the glass. The same treatment can be given to cracks in corrugated plastic roofing sheets.

31.   For masking areas prior to painting, be sure to use only masking tape – never cellophane tape. The masking tape has a special release adhesive which won't damage paint or paper, providing it is not left on too long.

32.   To hold furniture together while glue sets where the shape is not easy to clamp, use strips of old cycle inner tube. It moulds easily, holds firmly and it won't mark even the most delicate furniture.

33.   An idea as old as d-i-y itself, yet still useful, is to keep old screw top jars for storage. Fix the screw lids to the underside of a shelf and you don't take up valuable shelf space (*Figure 57*).

34. If shelves are spaced too wide apart, yet you don't want to add extra permanent shelving, make up simple shaped frames and merely stand them in place like little stools.

35. Make little hanging shelves for the inside of a larder door as shown in *Figure 58*. Be sure the hooks go into the door frame and not just into the thin skin which may cover it.

36. To stop carpets fraying at a cut, treat the back of the carpet with a liberal coating of carpet adhesive worked well into the backing. Give a final trim when the adhesive has set.

37. Off-cuts of laminate make useful cutting boards and table mats. Back with old cork wall or floor tiles stuck in place with rubber-based adhesive.

38. To make a dowel rod smaller, use a metal plate drilled with a hole of the required size. Hammer the dowel through the hole – or if the dowel has to be a lot smaller, hammer through a series of slightly smaller holes.

39. To get extra leverage on a screwdriver where a screw is hard to undo, clamp a self-grip wrench to the body of the screwdriver (*Figure 59*). Be careful not to turn off the screw head!

40. If you have to shape a ceramic tile – say to fit around a pipe – use a special tile file. Protect your eyes from any fine slivers of glaze which may fly off during filing.

41. When knocking a piece of wood in place which you don't want to bruise, and if you don't have a soft face hammer, use a rubber door stop between wood and hammer (*Figure 60*). Or use a piece of scrap wood and hit the scrap piece only.

42. Most power tools have too short a flex. Make up an extension cable, with unbreakable socket at one end and unbreakable plug at the other. Or you can buy one ready-made in many department stores these days.

43. Where only one socket outlet is available for your tools and you really need more, invest in a small distribution board with two or three socket outlets connected to a

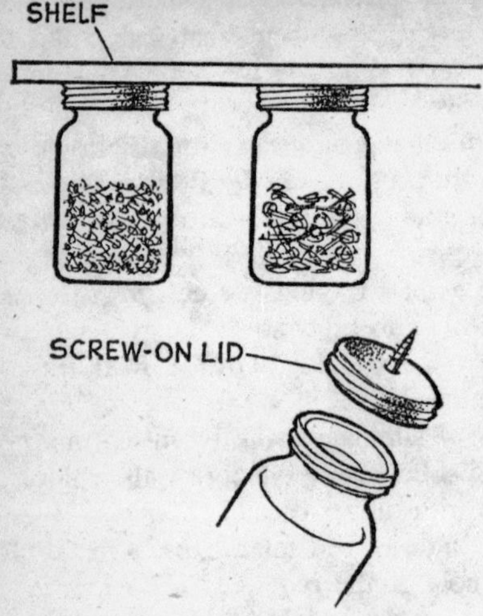

SIMPLE STORAGE SYSTEM

Figure 57

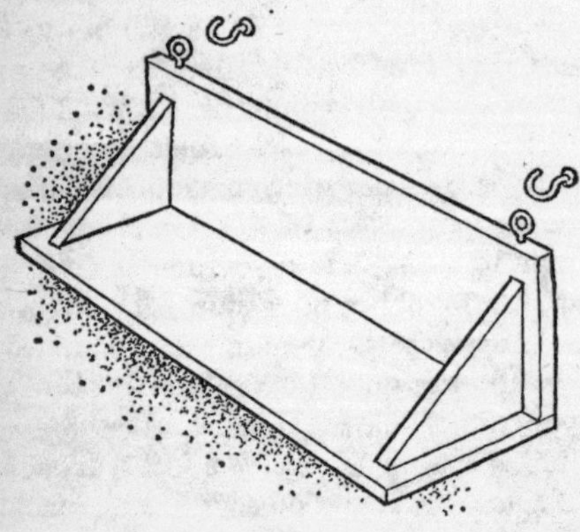

SIMPLE HOOK-ON SHELF

Figure 58

fused plug. Be sure to read the instructions as to the maximum load the board will carry.

44.   Don't trail spare flex – say to a standard lamp – under the carpet. Walking over it can damage the flex in time, perhaps causing a serious fire. Take the flex around the perimeter of the room – or have new socket outlets.

45.   If you dismantle any piece of equipment, make a little sketch of where parts go – and which way round. If

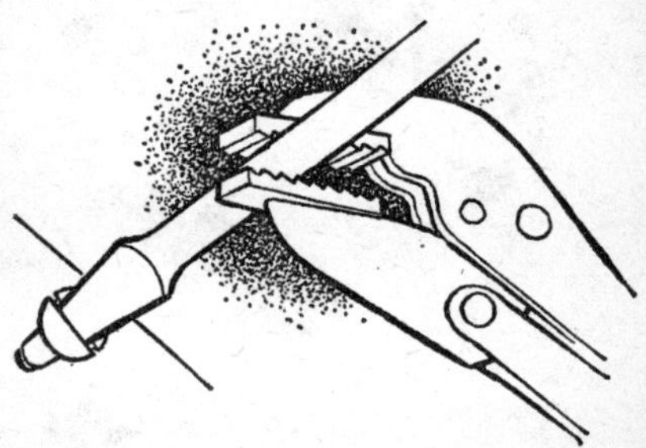

Figure 59

there are any gear wheels, mark with a pencil how they interlock. Such precautions can save hours of frustration. Store all loose parts in plastic bags until required.

46.   Never work near drains or above sink wastes, where small parts could drop down. Put small mechanisms inside a polythene bag when removing springs which could ping away, never to be seen again!

47.   Protect baths, basins and lavatory pans with plenty of cloth or towelling when removing taps or fittings. A dropped tap or spanner will very easily damage delicate surfaces.

48.   Remember to keep solvents, brush cleaners and abrasives well away from acrylic basins and baths. All will attack the highly finished surface, causing irreparable damage.

49.   Always open windows to ensure good ventilation when

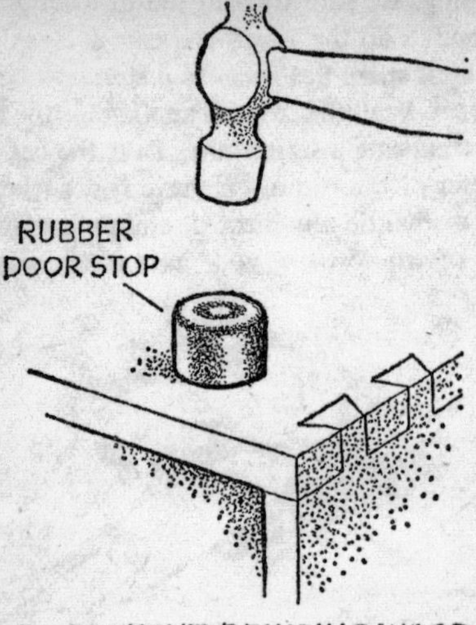

Figure 60

using adhesive containing solvents – especially flooring ones. If you wear overalls or old clothes, hang them out for a good airing after use. And make sure there are no naked flames in the vicinity – including gas pilot lights.

50. Never use petrol as a cleaning agent – except perhaps out in the open air under strictly controlled conditions. No smoking, or storing petrol in jam jars or paraffin cans.

6

Glossary of terms

Like all activities, do-it-yourself has a technical vocabulary which you just can't avoid. Most of it comes from the tradesman, and if you are reading articles, or ordering materials it will pay you to get to know the jargon! Below you will find listed the most common words together with a simple explanation.

Aggregate	The ingredients which are added to cement to produce concrete. Basically sand, stones of various sizes and gravel.
Air brick	A perforated brick set into a wall to allow good ventilation. The most important are those ventilating an underfloor area.
Amps (*ampères*)	A term representing the current flowing in an electrical cable. You will find it related to watts and volts. Amps = watts divided by volts.
Architrave	A moulding used to cover the gap between a joinery frame and the adjoining plaster.
Arris rail	A horizontal rail in a fence to which the fencing boards are nailed, usually slotted into the fence posts.
Ball float	A copper or plastic ball attached to the arm of a

           valve. It moves up and down with the water level in a tank, cutting off the water supply at a pre-determined level.

Ball valve   A special valve connected to a float, designed to admit or cut off water to a water storage tank.

Batten   A narrow piece of softwood. A typical use is as supports for slates or tiles on a roof.

Bay (concrete)   A way of dividing up a drive or path so that divisions are formed at given intervals. This reduces stresses, preventing cracking.

Bay (window)   A window which protrudes from a house wall. Usually a number of straight sections joined together to form a rectangle or curve.

Bending spring   This is used inside a piece of copper pipe to assist in bending the pipe without kinking it.

Blockboard   A rigid board made of battens sandwiched between veneers of plywood.

Breeze block   A lightweight, open structure building block, usually grey in colour, often found as the inner leaf of a cavity wall.

BS   An abbreviation for British Standard, to which many materials and products must conform.

Building paper   A waterproof material rather resembling brown paper. It may be reinforced with hessian, or have one or two reflective foil surfaces. Ideal for draughtproofing lofts.

Butted   Two or more surfaces which are pressed together without any form of jointing.

Cable   Non-flexible wires sheathed in plastic (in some cases metal), for carrying electrical power. At the time of writing, cable is still coloured black (neutral) and red (live).

Cable clip   Small device for supporting cable at regular intervals where it has to run horizontally on a surface.

Capillary joint   A simple method of joining copper pipe lengths. Solder is set inside the joining piece in the factory. Heating it causes the solder to flow by capillary action, making a permanent watertight joint.

Capstan head   The handle part of a tap which controls the flow of water. Usually held in place by a 'grub' screw.

Cartridge fuse   Fuse wire sealed inside a small cartridge. The most common cartridge fuses are used in fused 13 amp plugs, and are either 3 amp or 13 amp rating.

Casement stay   The metal bar used to control the movement of a casement window. Very often has holes to locate over a pin.

Cavity wall   A wall with an inner and an outer leaf, with a clear air gap in between. This prevents damp moving into the house. Today the gap may be filled with insulation to cut heat loss.

Ceiling rose   The fitting from which a suspended light is wired. It usually has a cover which unscrews to reveal the fixing points.

Chipboard   A building and construction board made of fine wood chips bonded together with a resin-like material. It may be bought plain, or with surfaces veneered with wood or plastic.

Circuit breaker   A protective device installed in an electrical circuit to break the circuit if overloading occurs. It can be reset once any fault has been corrected.

Cladding   A covering material, either over a framework, or as a decorative finish to masonry.

Closeboard   The type of fencing where each board overlaps its neighbour to give a completely unbroken surface.

Cockspur   The handle used to keep shut a casement window. Often used in conjunction with a casement stay.

Colour code   Domestically, it means the colouring of electrical wires. Black (neutral) and red (live) for cables; and blue (neutral), brown (live) and yellow/green (earth) for flexes.

Compression joint   A type of pipe joint where a seal is made by tightening a nut or nuts with a spanner. Not as neat as a capillary joint, but easier for the amateur to make.

Conduit   A metal or plastic piping through which electrical cable is run to switches and socket outlets.

Connector   A means of joining together electrical wires, giving a much more positive and safe joint than twisting wires together.

Consumer unit   A neat modern way of grouping together all the fuses needed for house wiring circuits. It replaces the old style fuse boxes.

Coping   The top course of masonry or brickwork, usually sloped so that rain runs off.

Cord pull   Usually associated with a type of switch operated by a cord. Used in bathrooms for lights and electric fires so there is no chance of wet hands touching a switch direct.

Cove or coving   In d-i-y terms usually refers to the decorative cove cornice which bridges the gap between wall and ceiling.

Damp proof course (dpc)   A horizontal barrier built into a wall to prevent damp rising above a certain point. Many older properties have no dpc.

Dash   A decorative wall surfacing of pebbles or chips of spar produced by 'dashing' them against a wet rendering.

Deadlock   A type of lock where once the key has been turned and removed, the mechanism is 'dead' and cannot be operated without the key.

Door chain   Designed to prevent a door opening more than a few inches. It cannot be released until the door has been shut. Used as a security device against unwanted callers.

Double insulated Any appliance where the electrical parts are isolated from the user, and no earth wire is required, is referred to as double insulated. It is indicated by a box within a box symbol displayed on the appliance.

Dowel   A timber or metal rod or peg used to join two or more pieces of wood together. Various dowelling jigs are available to assist with joint making.

Downpipe   The rainwater pipes which take water away from the gutters. They usually consist of a number of sections slotted together.

Drain cock — A special tap at the very lowest point of a plumbing system or radiator circuit so that the water can be drained off.

Earthed — Any appliance which is connected to earth by means of its wiring and the socket to which it is connected. It is a safety route for stray electricity, rather than passing through you to the ground.

Earth wire — The wire which connects the casing of an appliance to earth in case of a fault developing in the appliance.

Eaves — The gap between the fascia board to which gutters are fixed, and the tiles or slates on the roofs. Where birds like to nest.

Efflorescence — A whitish deposit which comes from masonry, often as damp dries out. Caused by chemicals in the bricks or blocks. It can be neutralised by chemical treatment.

Expanded polystyrene — Polystyrene plastic which has been foamed until it is about ninety-eight per cent air. Used widely for insulation and for packaging.

Expansion pipe — A pipe in the plumbing system which allows for any expansion of water in the system, and which would take water away if it happened to boil.

Expansion tank — A small tank holding a reservoir of water for a central heating system, and to allow for any expansion of the water in the central heating system.

Extension cable — An electrical cable with socket and plug to allow any electrical appliance to reach further. It always has a socket at the end delivering the power.

Fascia board — The board to which rainwater gutter brackets are fixed. Located just below the eaves.

Flashing — A lead or composition sheet material used to seal the gap between two surfaces – such as the joint between a chimney stack and the tiles or slates through which the stack passes.

Flaunching A cement mortar layer into which chimney pots are set at the top of the chimney stack.

Flex The flexible type of cable used for domestic appliances where it must be able to bend freely. Not to be confused with cable which must not be 'flexed'.

Flue The means by which waste gases are taken away from a fire or boiler.

Fuse The weak link in an electrical circuit which is designed to melt if a fault develops either by short circuit or overloading.

Fuse box The container in which the various circuit fuses are housed. In modern homes, replaced by a consumer unit.

Fuse wire The special wire used to bridge the connections of the old type fuse carriers. It varies in thickness according to the circuit it protects.

Galvanising A special zinc coating applied to metal to prevent rust or corrosion. It is factory applied to items like window frames and corrugated metal sheeting. A special galvanising paint is available for coating metal which hasn't been galvanised.

Gland nut The nut on a tap which compresses the gland packing, to stop water getting out of the tap by way of the tap spindle.

Gland packing A fibrous material used to pack around a tap spindle to prevent water getting out. An emergency replacement is knitting wool and Vaseline.

Glass fibre Glass especially spun to form a cotton wool like material. It is used mainly for insulation, but it can be woven into cloth to make fire blankets, or provided as a tape for reinforcing repair materials. Curtains are also available woven from glass fibre.

Glazing sprig A small headless tack designed to hold glass in a frame. Metal frames often have glazing clips.

Grommet A special protective device, usually of rubber, which prevents damage to a flexible cable at the point at which it joins the appliance or passes into an appliance.

Grub screw A tiny securing screw which goes down into a threaded hole. You will find a grub screw holding a tap handle to the spindle.

Gulley An open area into which sink and basin water discharges. One good reason for its use is that should sewage be forced back up the drains, it would only move as far as the gulley – not up into the sink.

Gutter The collecting point on any roof for rainwater before it is passed to the down pipes. Gutters can be of metal or plastic.

Hasp and staple The two pieces of hardware fitted to a gate or door so that a padlock can be used to secure it. The simplest hasp and staple offers very little security.

Hit and miss ventilator A ventilator which has a perforated shutter which can be opened or closed to control ventilation.

Hopper The wide open end of a down-pipe into which bath and basin waste water discharges. A weak spot in freezing weather.

Housing A slot cut into a piece of timber, across the wood grain, into which another piece of timber will be fitted.

Inspection chamber The area under the metal covers around the house from which the drains can be examined and cleaned.

Joints Different methods of fixing two or more items together. Mostly encountered in woodworking.

Joists The horizontal timbers in the house to which ceilings and floors are secured.

Jumper The little piece inside a tap to which the washer is fitted. It is free to move up and down as the tap handle is turned.

Junction box A box in which electrical wires meet, are joined and routed elsewhere in an electrical circuit.

KD An abbreviation now widely used for furniture in

	kit form. It comes in 'knock down' condition for home assembly.
Key	Apart from its obvious meaning, it also means roughing a surface so that another material will stick to it. May be used in plasterwork, rendering and painting articles. And when using some adhesives you roughen the surface to give a good 'key'.
Keyhole plate	A metal or plastic plate fitted over the hole cut in a door to take the key. Can be fitted with a key-hole flap.
Knot	A hard coloured area in a piece of wood where a branch was once joined. Looks decorative as long as it is not loose.
Lath and plaster	The traditional old way of making a ceiling. Laths nailed to the joists were coated in plaster.
Leaf	A term used for one section of a cavity wall. The inner leaf or the outer leaf.
Lintel	A specially strong beam designed to support brickwork. You will see them over window openings and doors.
Loadbearing	Used mainly in reference to walls designed to carry weight from above. A partition is non-loadbearing.
Mains pressure	Any tap or plumbing fitting supplied with water direct from the mains supply is said to be at mains pressure. The alternative is storage tank pressure.
Mains switch	An electrical switch connected to the mains which, when in the off position, cuts the supply to the whole house.
Mastic	A sealing compound which retains its flexibility even when set. Ideal around windows and doors where there may be slight movement.
Mat well	A recessed area near an external door into which a mat will fit.
Meter	A device for measuring electricity or gas so that payment may be calculated.

Mineral wool An insulating material formed by melting and spinning natural rock. It resembles dirty cotton wool. It won't burn.

Mirror plate A small metal plate screwed to the back of a mirror or small cabinet by which it is fixed to the wall.

Mortar A buttery mix of cement, sand and often lime used for bricklaying, block laying and repair work.

Mortise A hole cut into a piece of wood into which a tenon joint will fit. Or it may be a hole cut to take a mortise lock.

Mortise lock A lock set right into the edge of a door so that only the latch and bolt protrude.

Muntins The vertical and horizontal rails in a window which divide it into smaller panes.

Newel post The vertical post top and bottom of a staircase supporting the rail.

Nosing The projecting part of a stair tread, usually rounded.

Opening light That part of a casement window designed to open.

Overflow pipe A pipe connected to a tank or cistern to take away water should the valve fail. It must be able to take away water faster than it could be fed in.

Overload Usually referred to an electrical circuit where too many high wattage appliances are connected. This will cause the fuse to melt, protecting the circuit.

Partition A dividing wall often erected after a house has been built. It carries no load from above.

Party wall The wall you share with your neighbour if you live in a semi-detached or terraced house.

Peephole viewer A small lens system which enables an occupier to look out at any visitor without being seen. Used for security.

Pendant fitting Any light fitting hanging down. May also refer to a switch.

Picture hook	A double ended hook designed to grip a picture rail for picture hanging. Now often replaced by picture pins.
Plasterboard	A building board made of plaster faced with a tough paper liner. It is widely used in house construction in place of traditional plastering. Also used for partitioning.
Plate glass	A thick, accurately polished glass used for large windows, shelves and table tops.
Plunger cup	A rubber or plastic cup designed to fit over a sink or basin waste, to clear a blockage. When agitated, a pressure is created in the waste pipe which clears most blockages.
Plywood	A construction board which is very strong and pliable. It is made of wood veneers laid one upon the other, each at right angles to its neighbour.
Pointing	The finishing of the mortar joint between brickwork. This mortar may crumble and need scraping out and repointing.
P trap	You will find a trap fitted to sink and basin wastes and lavatory pans to stop smells and prevent draughts. The P trap is one pattern, named after its shape. The alternative is the S trap – also named after its shape.
Quadrant moulding	A strip of wood used for decoration. It forms a quarter of the circumference of a circle.
Rafters	The roof timbers which give support for the roof covering – usually slates or tiles.
Rails	The main horizontal sections of a window or door. Also used to describe the track upon which curtain runners move.
Rebate	A step cut into or along a piece of wood into which another piece may fit. You may also see it called a rabbet.
Rendering	A coating of plaster on an inside wall or of cement mortar on an outside wall. An external rendering is usually decorated with a masonry paint.

Ridge	The very top or peak of a sloping roof where the roof faces meet.
Ridge tiles	The row of tiles which cap the roof where the roof faces meet.
Ring main	The modern method of wiring socket outlets by connecting them to a ring of cable.
Riser	The vertical member of a stair upon which rests the tread.
Rising main	The water pipe bringing the water into a house from the mains pipe in the road. It rises to the storage tank in the loft.
Rose	The electrical fitting on a ceiling to which is connected a pendant light.
RPM	An abbreviation for revolutions per minute, usually referring to the speed of an electric motor or a spindle geared from the motor.
RSJ	An abbreviation for rolled steel joist – used to hold up or strengthen part of a building.
Sash cord	The rope connected to a weight which supports a sliding sash window. There will be a cord either side of a sash.
Sash window	A window which opens and closes by sliding up and down.
Screed	A very thin layer of cement-based material designed to level an uneven floor. You will also see it called a screeding compound.
Screen blocks	Blocks cast from concrete, having one of a variety of open patterns. They offer a garden screen, but still let light and air through.
Scrim	A material rather resembling a bandage used with plaster to bridge joints in a plasterboard wall. It adds strength and helps prevent cracking of the plaster.
Seating	The surface inside a tap on to which the tap washer presses to cut off the water. Taps can drip because of a damaged seating.
Sewer	The big pipe into which domestic waste is drained.

Shingles	Split timber tiles, usually of western red cedar, mainly used for decorating external walls.
Short circuit	A fault which allows electricity to pass to earth without passing through the correct circuit. It should result in a fuse blowing to make the circuit safe.
Shuttering	A timber frame built up into which concrete is tipped. The most common application you will meet is in path and drive construction.
Skirting board	The board which hides the gap between a wall and a floor, and which takes the knocks from furniture.
Sleeper walls	Small walls under a timber floor which support the floor joists.
Soakaway	A special pit filled with rubble into which rain-water is drained when there is no piped system.
Socket outlet	The part of an electrical circuit into which appliance plugs are inserted.
Soil vent pipe	A pipe which rises to roof level, carrying away foul air from the lavatory waste pipe.
Spigot	The plain end of a pipe fitting into the socket of another.
Sprig	See glazing sprig.
Spur	A branch taken from a ring circuit to feed further socket outlets.
Stair well	The open area enclosed by a staircase.
Stile	The vertical members of a door or window.
Stipple	A texture or pattern produced by dabbing a surface. It may be done by a sponge, crumpled rag or paper, or brush.
Stop cock	A tap located on a water pipe by means of which the flow may be cut off.
Stop tap	Usually the tap under the sink or in a nearby cupboard used to cut the mains water supply. There will also be a stop tap near the pavement which the water authority can use to cut a supply.
Straining wire	A wire pulled very tight to hold something in

	place. You will often find them used in wire fencing to hold the fencing taut.
S trap	The trap, fitted to sink and basin wastes and lavatory pans to stop smells and prevent draughts, which has an S shape. The alternative is the **P** trap – also named after its shape.
Striker plate	The plate on a door frame which houses the latch or bolt of a door lock.
Strip light	A tubular lamp with a filament running horizontally through it. Used in bedside lights and over mirrors.
Swan neck	A long curving tap spout which resembles the neck of a swan.
Tamping board	A length of timber used to work concrete into place by moving it up and down and from side to side.
Template	A shape cut from card or thin metal which is used to trace the shape on to another material to ensure accurate fitting.
Thermostat	A sensitive instrument for controlling temperature. As it reacts to temperature changes it can be used to switch on or off some form of heating.
Threshold	The area immediately below a door frame, usually shaped as a projecting step.
Throat	The gap immediately above a fireplace opening up which the smoke and fumes pass into the flue. This gap is often made smaller by a throat restrictor.
Time clock	A clock with adjustable tabs which can be used to switch on and off an electrical circuit. It may control a central heating system, electric fire, lamp or radio.
Tongue and groove	A way of joining boards together by fitting a tongue on one board into a groove in another. Often used for joining floorboards.
Traps	See P trap and S trap.
Tread	That part of a stair upon which you tread and which is supported by the riser.

Tubular heater	A black heat heater resembling a length of sealed pipe in which there is an electrical element. It gives a gentle heat and consumes little more electricity than a light bulb.
U bend	The U-shaped section of waste pipe under a sink or basin which holds enough water to make a seal and prevent smells and draughts coming up the waste pipe.
Underlay	An under-carpet of felt or foam rubber upon which the main carpet lies. It improves the comfort, and extends the life of any carpet.
Valance	A short curtain around a frame, a bed or above a hanging curtain. It may be hung from a valance rail.
Veneer	A thin shaving of decorative wood often used to decorate a less attractive base material. Veneers are also used in marquetry work.
Ventilation brick	A perforated brick set into a wall to allow air to circulate freely. Most commonly used to ventilate under-floor areas of a house.
Vermiculite	An expanded material consisting of lightweight granules, widely used for insulating loft spaces.
Vertical tiling	Tiling used to decorate exterior walls while giving added protection to the wall.
Volts	A term representing the pressure of an electrical supply. In Britain it is between 200 and 240 volts. You will find it related to amps and watts. Volts = watts divided by amps.
Wall tie	A small device, usually of metal, which anchors the two leaves of a wall together at regular intervals. They are added to a wall during its construction.
Washer	The small replaceable part of a tap which makes a seal on the tap seating and cuts off the water.
Waste pipe	The pipe used to carry waste away from sinks and basins and lavatory pans.
Watts	A term representing the amount of electricity in a

circuit. You will find it related to amps and volts. Watts = amps multiplied by volts.

Weatherboard   A timber cladding used on the outside of a house. Today it is mainly a decorative surface.

Zinc rich paint   A paint used to apply a cold galvanising coat to metal. It effectively prevents rusting.

Index

adhesive types   32
anaglypta   36

ball floats   104
ball valves   103
ball valve types   102
blockboard   40
blowtorch, using   48
bolts, rusted   125
burglar alarms   110

cabinet fixing   75
cable colours   93
callers, unwelcome   116
carpets, creeping   123
carpet fray, preventing   129
cavity infill   83
ceiling painting   66
ceiling papering   61
ceiling tile painting   67
central heating   105
ceramic tile drilling   125

chipboard   40
condensation problems   88
coving fixing   63
coving types   63
cramps   8
cupboard, fixing to wall   73
curtain rails sticking   124

damp, dealing with   85
damp proof course, faulty   87
damp, where it enters   86
decorating   45
door bolts   109
door chain   107
door locks   107
double glazing   84
double insulation   97
drains blocked   116
draughtproofing   80
drawer runners sticking   124

dry rot   89
duplex papers   36

electrics   91
emergencies   111
emergency kit   112
extension cable   98

fillers   30
fillers, using   52
fire in chip pan   114
fire in house   114
floors, condensation   85
floors, damp   85
floors, smoothing   67
flue damp   91
furniture fittings   72
furniture renovating   69
furniture repairs   71
fuse checking   94
fuse ratings   94
fuse types   92

gas leaks   106, 113
gas supply   106
gland packing   103
glass laminate for security   109
glass, temporary repairs   128
glossary of useful terms   133
   (These are alphabetical, so
   are not indexed individually)
gutters leaking   87

hardboard   41
heat losses   81
hinge bolts   109

hints and tips   121
home security   107

insulation   80
insulation, gap filling   82
insulation, lofts   82
insulation, walls   83
iron flex replacing   97

knotting   28

laminate fixing   79
laminates   42
laminboard   40
light failure   113
lining paper   38
locked out   115
locks, lubricating   124

machines, oiling   124
masking tape, using   128
mastics   31
mould caused by damp   89

nail removing   124
nail types   18
nailing thin wood   128
nursery paint   70

paint, applying   54
paint kettle   121
paint, measuring for   23
paint pads   57
paint rollers   56
paint skinning   121
paint spills   119
paint straining   121
paint stripping   46

paint types 25
paintbrushes 53
paintbrush storing 122
petrol, care with 132
pipes frozen 119
plastic sheet, self-adhesive 43
plug wiring 96
plumbing 98
plumbing traps 104
plumbing, trap types 105
plywood 40
polythene sheet joining 126
primer 28
putty 30
pvc repairs 128

roofing check 87
rugs and mats slipping 123
rust loosening 124

screeding compound 68
screw types 18
screw loosening 124
sealants 31
security devices 108
shelving, fixing 74
shelving ideas 77
solvents, care with 132
stains and seals 29
steam wallpaper stripping 49
stop taps 99
stopping 30

tacks, holding 126
tapes 31, 35
tap types 101
tap washer replacing 100
taps 100
taps, dripping 100
thermostats 105
throw-away brushes 126
tile cutting 65
tile shaping 65
tiles, vinyl, scuff marks 125
tiles, ceiling, removing 51
tiles, ceramic, fixing 64
tiles, floor, removing 52
tiles, measuring for 25
tiles, various 43
timber choosing 39
time clocks 106
tools, basic kit 10, 15
tools, correct use 5
tools, cutting 11
tools, drilling 13
tools, driving 13
tools, gripping and turning 14
tools, hiring 17
tools, hitting 12
tools, measuring 9
tools, power 16
tools, shaping 12

undercoats 29

veneer insulation 39
veneered chipboard 41
ventilation 84
vices 8
vinyl wallcoverings 37
vinyl wallcovering seams 123

wallcovering, measuring for 24
wallcovering, pre-pasted 60
wallcovering, special effects 38
wallpaper, applying 58
wallpaper, cutting 122
wallpaper, greasy marks 119
wallpaper matching 61
wallpaper painting 50
wallpaper stripping 49
wallpaper tearing 122
wallpaper trimming 60
wallpapers 36
wall plug types 76
walls, damp 87
waste outlets 104
water leaks 113

RESTORATION AND REPAIR
A Handbook for Use at Home

Michéle Brown

Do you have a chair which needs recaning, or some broken china to be mended, or some pictures to be re-framed?

This book is to help you care for, and repair where necessary, all those things which together furnish your home. There is advice on everyday running repairs, such as removing heat stains from wood, but also explanations of advanced skills such as replacing a small patch of veneer.

All the techniques included can successfully be carried out at home and will both save you costly repair bills and provide you with the satisfaction of having done the job yourself.

Topics covered include furniture restoration, picture framing, the care and repair of books, china and glass and there is also a section on materials needing special care, such as marble and alabaster.

TEACH YOURSELF BOOKS

HOUSE REPAIRS

Tony Wilkins

Buying a house is probably the biggest financial outlay you will ever make. However, if this asset is not to become a liability, a continuous programme of repair and maintenance is of great importance. Neglect soon leads to an increasing number of problems and general deterioration of the fabric.

The problems you meet will, of course, vary according to the type of property you have but, whatever they are, you can make considerable financial savings by dealing with them yourself.

This book will both help you to identify trouble spots and provide you with the knowledge to enable you to do a good job. A summary of the problems you might find, both inside and outside the house, is followed by a reference section of advice on how to tackle them. Topics covered include the roof, doors, windows, walls, damp, house surrounds, floors, ceilings, drainage.

TEACH YOURSELF BOOKS